Ask and Tell: Self-Advocacy and Disclosure for People on the Autism Spectrum

Ask and Tell: Self-Advocacy and Disclosure for People on the Autism Spectrum

Edited by
Stephen M. Shore

Foreword by
Temple Grandin

Autism Asperger Publishing Co.
P.O. Box 23173
Shawnee Mission, KS 66283-0173
www.asperger.net

© 2004 Autism Asperger Publishing Co.
P.O. Box 23173
Shawnee Mission, KS 66283-0173
www.asperger.net

Publisher's Cataloging-in-Publication
(Provided by Quality Books, Inc.)

Ask and tell : self-advocacy and disclosure for people on
    the autism spectrum / edited by Stephen Shore ; foreword
    by Temple Grandin.
        p. cm.
        Includes bibliographical references and index.
        Library of Congress Control Number: 2004106924
        ISBN 1-931282-58-7

        1. Autism–Patients. 2. Autism–Patients–
Rehabilitation. 3. Autism–Social aspects. 4. Autism–
Political aspects. I. Shore, Stephen M., 1961-

RC553.A88A85 2004   616.85′882
                      QBI33-2041

This book is designed in Palatino and Helvetica Neue.

Managing Editor: Kirsten McBride
Editorial Assistance: Ginny Biddulph

Cover: "1,000 Cranes" by Jose Estevez of the Higashi School of Greater Boston. The artist's unique vision of creating 1,000 origami cranes from a Japanese legend is offered as a symbol of world peace and hope for the future.

Printed in the United States of America

With profound appreciation and deep gratitude,
we dedicate this book to

our mentors – past, present and future.

May you, dear reader, benefit from the generosity
of true allies and mentors and,
in turn, teach and nurture others.

ACKNOWLEDGMENTS

This book was made possible with the assistance and encouragement of many people who believed in the worth and value of this project. First and foremost among these are my fellow contributors, Ruth Elaine Hane, Roger Meyer, Phil Schwarz, Kassiane Sibley, and Liane Willey, all of whom have toiled tirelessly on this endeavor from the very beginning.

Gratitude is also in order to dear friends such as Jean-Paul Bovee, Thomas Cottle, Ph.D., my "younger sister" Sandy and family, Frank, Frankie, and Lisa D'Erasmo, Gerald Fain, Ph.D., Dena Gassner, MSW, Neal Goodman, Dania Jekel, MSW, Sarah and Steven Knudsen, Stephanie Loo, Jerry Newport, Karen and Sam Pandolfi, Cathy, Jerry, and Zachariah Silbert, Eileen Torchio, and Temple Grandin. The work of Amanda Baggs, Michelle Dawson, Frank Klein, Jane Meyerding, Clare Sainsbury, Jim Sinclair, and Valerie Paradiz has also significantly contributed to this project.

All of my work in the area of people with differences is only possible through the unconditional love, acceptance, and support from my Mom and Dad, siblings, Robin and Martin, all of my grandparents, and my wife, Yi Liu, all of whom have been a continuing course of strength to me. To those whom I have inadvertently left out of this acknowledgment, only to remember them after this book goes into print, please accept my apologies along with my heartfelt thanks

Special thanks also to the Autism Society of America, on whose board of directors I currently serve. We appreciate ASA's encouragement and resources for the six contributors of this book to hold an all-day workshop on self-advocacy and disclosure during the 2003 national conference in Pittsburgh, Pennsylvania. In particular, Cathy Pratt suggested that rather than my original idea of presenting on classroom accommodations we do "something directly for people on the autism spectrum."

As part of our efforts towards teaching self-advocacy and disclosure, many thanks are in order to the Higashi School of Greater Boston, directed by Robert Fantasia, for providing the artwork for the cover just as they did for my earlier book, *Beyond the Wall: Personal Experiences with Autism and Asperger Syndrome*. Mr. Akihiro Takamatsu (Mr. T.) suggested to Jose Estevez that he draw the cranes for the cover. Mr. T. is one of the few remaining original members of the Higashi School staff from Japan who brought Daily Life Therapy to the United States as developed by Dr. Kiyo Kitahara in Tokyo.

Finally, I wish to express my appreciation for the wonderful managerial, editing and support from my editor, Kirsten McBride. Her help in bringing our six contributions into a unified whole that is greater than the sum of its parts was immeasurable.

– Stephen Shore

Contents

FOREWORD

Temple Grandin

This book provides an abundance of useful information that will help people with high-functioning autism and Asperger Syndrome navigate their way through the public school system, learn social rules and ultimately advocate for themselves. It also explores the degrees of disclosure and whether or not self-disclosure is a good choice, depending upon the situation and the individual's personality and preferences.

The autism spectrum is broad-ranging, from those who are nonverbal to brilliant scientists. There are also intermediate types such as persons who are fully verbal but have very rigid speech. Others on the spectrum have sensory problems that are so severe that they cannot function in a typical office environment, for example, unless modifications are made in lighting or noise levels.

Whether or not it is appropriate to disclose a diagnosis of autism or Asperger varies, depending upon the severity of the person's problems. Usually, in order to function successfully, people with severe sensory sensitivities, for example, have to disclose that they need an office that is free of fluorescent lights. In come cases, it may be better to tell the employer that fluorescent lights cause headaches instead of attempting to teach the employer about Asperger Syndrome. Individuals with more obvious symptoms such as extremely rigid-sounding speech are probably better off with full disclosure.

However, there are other times when disclosure is not appropriate. I once visited a small company that employed 28 computer and technical people who made specialized electronic equipment with finely machined parts. It was a little enclave of Aspies. In that situation, I did not think that it was appropriate to tell them about Asperger Syndrome. They were functioning well and successfully selling their products around the world. I decided to leave them in peace in their building in an industrial park somewhere in the United States. It is a nice little Asperger community that does not know they have Asperger Syndrome and for whom contact with the formal autism/Asperger world would not be helpful.

There are two groups in the Asperger community – the ones who know they have Asperger Syndrome and those who do not. In technical fields there are many Asperger people who perform well in their jobs, but many are not doing so well in their personal lives. This book will be immensely helpful for their personal lives because now their spouse or relatives will better understand some of their unique characteristics and challenges.

At autism meetings I am seeing more and more individuals who have mild forms of Asperger Syndrome. In my job designing livestock equipment, I see many similar people employed as draftsmen, welders, research scientists, or computer specialists. There is no black or white dividing line between "computer nerd" and Asperger's. In many cases these people do not need to disclose that they have Asperger Syndrome. They just need to make themselves so good at their jobs that they are appreciated for their talents. In my own case, I rarely tell clients I am autistic. Equipment I have designed is used by every major meat company in the United States. People thought I was weird, but they appreciated my work. Clients find out about my autism when they have a friend with an autistic child. When this happens, I end up doing autism consulting at a meat packing plant instead of designing equipment. For the first 10 years of my career, I did not do any disclosure until my first book, *Emergence, Labeled Autistic*, was published in 1986.

As mentioned throughout this book, in some cases it is advisable for persons with autism spectrum disorders to find a mentor at work who can help them navigate the social minefields. Also, *The Wall Street Journal* has many good articles to help people deal with mean bosses or sexual harassment.

For those who have mild Asperger Syndrome, the main thing is to develop and sell their talent. Early in my career I was livestock editor for the *Arizona Farmer Ranchman* magazine. When the magazine was sold, the new owner wanted to fire me because he thought I was weird. I saved my job by making a portfolio of all my articles. When the new boss saw my good work, he decided to keep me.

People on the spectrum have to be on the lookout for jealous co-workers who may sabotage them. I have had problems in this area. If the person causing you problems is your boss, you are in trouble, but if it is a co-worker, I have found it best to avoid conflict. Over the years I have learned to be more diplomatic. I learned early in my career that telling others that they were stupid is an almost sure way to lose a job!

I think the best way individuals on the spectrum can advocate for themselves is to sell their strengths. We need to tell the world about the things we are good at, such as being hard workers who can get a specialized job done. People on the spectrum are good at specialized things, and talents need to be developed in the specific areas that others find valuable, such as drafting, accounting, scientific research, and fixing things such as cars or computers. Skills are usually uneven in people on the spectrum – they are good at one thing and not so good at something else.

The emphasis needs to be on the talents, not the deficits. After all, the really social people did not invent the first stone spear – they were too busy chatting around the fire. Throughout history, it has been the Asperger-type people who have given us such things as electricity, for example.

The best advocacy is to work with local businesses, agencies, and schools to sell people on the Asperger person's strengths. Talents such as art, music or science must be encouraged in young children so their skills can turn into rewarding careers. In my own life, I have found that the happiest times have been in construction projects, talking about "cool stuff' we were building. It was "techie"-to-"techie" talk, and to me it provided rewarding social interaction.

I have observed that the people with Asperger Syndrome who have rewarding, fulfilling lives share three common factors: development of talents, mentors at school and at work, and treatment for anxiety and sensory problems. Anxiety would have destroyed me, but antidepressant medication saved me. Some Asperger individuals do not need medication, but others will be miserable without either medical or dietary treatment. This is one area where people on the spectrum need to advocate for services so that they can get the appropriate treatment. There is a great need for more doctors who are knowledgeable about autism spectrum disorders. Another area where people need to advocate is health insurance. Many of the niche jobs where Asperger individuals are hired offer little or no health insurance.

– Temple Grandin
Associate Professor, Department of Animal Science
Colorado State University

INTRODUCTION

Stephen M. Shore

Leading a fulfilling and productive life involves maximizing control of one's destiny. By focusing on our strengths and what brings us satisfaction to accommodate for challenges we can build a stronger, more positive sense of self that benefits not only ourselves but our community as well. Being productive and fulfilled requires the ability to effectively make our preferences and needs known to others. To do so, in turn, requires a heightened sense of self-awareness – we must come to grips with who we are and what our needs are before we can communicate them to others.

Self-advocacy involves knowing when and how to approach others in order to negotiate desired goals, and to build better mutual understanding, fulfillment, and productivity. In the process, some degree of disclosure about oneself is usually necessary as we have to disclose the reasons why we are requesting a given accommodation, for example. Inevitably, this carries some degree of vulnerability along with the risk of rejection and failure – depending on the individual and the given situation. Yet, without embracing the twin issues of self-advocacy and disclosure, we face an even greater risk: living unfulfilled lives and depriving communities and society as a whole of the potential for people on the autism spectrum to make significant contributions. Despite the importance of effective self-advocacy and disclosure for individuals on the autism spectrum, for whom these behaviors usually do not develop as a matter of course, to date little attention has been paid towards developing such skills.

There are two compelling aspects that make this work especially relevant to the autistic community, allies, and others. First, all contributions – from the design of the cover, the foreword, and the body of this text – are by people on the autism spectrum. Second, this is the first book entirely devoted to the important twin issues of self-advocacy and disclosure for people with autism spectrum disorders. These two unique attributes combine to create a powerful work created by those who know best what their self-advocacy and disclosure needs are.

Socrates' statement that "the unexamined life is not worth living" encourages a systematic analysis of our lives as a major prerequisite for living fully in all areas of our existence. Given that systematic analysis is something that many people on the autism spectrum do very well, we encourage you to harness that strength by using the hard-earned advice presented by the contributors to this book.

Ask and Tell: Self-Advocacy and Disclosure for People on the Autism Spectrum opens with a very insightful chapter on how to integrate knowledge of self and learning about others so as to become better communicators. Given the challenges people on the autism spectrum face in reading facial expressions and other nonverbal communication, Ruth Elaine Hane provides a powerful, yet simple template for decoding this mode of communication and, therefore, allowing us to interact more successfully with others. In the following chapter, Kassiane Sibley details a six-step process for helping the young advocate-to-be gradually move toward independent self-advocacy and disclosure. My contribution, Chapter 3, suggests ways to use the individualized education program (IEP) to develop skills in self-advocacy and disclosure by involving students to the fullest extent of their ability in creating their own customized education. Skills learned through meaningful involvement in the IEP can be transferred to life after graduation.

Many of us will have contact with public and private social service agencies at various points in our lives. Roger Meyer provides practical tips on navigating an often Byzantine maze of forms, personnel, and even proper demeanor and dress, when interfacing with these agencies to build one's own "Individual Life Plan." Coming from an Aspie who has been on both sides of the table, the honest, often hard-hitting suggestions in this chapter are particularly helpful. Taking a slightly different slant on self-advocacy and disclosure, Phil Schwarz focuses on the community level by looking at how we can engage nonautistic people as our allies and together effect positive change in the larger society. Liane Willey wraps up the book by introducing several ways of self-disclosing, offering options that are suitable for most personalities and preferences – from the very subtle to the more direct – along with the importance of self-awareness combined with educating oneself and others about the autism spectrum.

Moving from specific examples and practical steps on the individual level to effecting change at the community level, this book aims to help people on the autism spectrum self-advocate more effectively in their pursuit of independent, productive, and fulfilling lives.

This book is one small effort by six autistic people focused on empowering individuals on the autism spectrum, their community and allies to join hands to achieve more meaningful, productive and fulfilling lives for the greater good of society.

CHAPTER 1

Communicating Through Advocacy and Self-Disclosure: Four Ways to Connect

Ruth Elaine Joyner Hane

Carol Lou and I practice calling one another on our home made tele phone so we can qualify for a Girl Scout badge. We tie knots in wrapping cord, passing the string through nail holes punched in the bottom of tin cans. I stand near the front of our single-car garage, as Carol Lou tromps past wildflowers blooming behind the lap-sided building long in need of repair. As she holds the tin can over her ear, I place mine over my mouth, the string pulling taut.

*"Hello? Do we have a connection? **Can you hear me?**" I call into my tin can.*

"What did you say, Ruth-E?" Carol Lou shouts back.

*"I said, **hear me?**"*

The cord breaks. We've lost our connection.

Communication over a hand-built telephone frequently ends in a lost connection. A similar thing happens whenever we talk and either the sender (talker) or the receiver (listener) has a problem picking up or "reading" the signals. The connection may be lost or compromised.

Successful communication is an even exchange, a rhythm of give and take, connecting with others in a respectful dance of listening and talking. Most people on the spectrum of autism are challenged with social communication, interaction and relationships. Social cues are sometimes overlooked or disregarded, causing misunderstanding and interpersonal challenges. Often, friendships are nonexistent, or if they do exist, they are functional rather than intimate. Frequently people within the spectrum of autism prefer to relate to objects rather than people, gathering and storing extensive amounts of information about things or about narrow, focused topics. Sometimes we have difficulty taking the perspective of others, maintaining eye-to-eye contact, and understanding nonverbal body language.

This chapter is a guide to learning how to communicate more effectively, to begin taking the steps in the dance of effective communication – a significant prerequisite for ultimately engaging in self-advocacy and disclosure, the overreaching topic of this book.

The discussion is divided into four areas of focus – *connections*. Just like the schematic layouts for electronic boards, successful communication follows an orderly system. Most neurotypicals, people not affected by autism, learn the system or dance more or less instinctively, whereas those of us on the autism spectrum need direct instruction and training in the intricacies of the connections that must be made to communicate effectively. Specifically, in the following pages we will look at sending clear signals, becoming aware of body language, defining our needs and wants and, finally, doing the dance – putting it all together.

Connection One: Sending Clear Signals

In effective communication, the signal from the sender is clear, and the receiver is open and receptive to hearing it. Becoming aware of our emotions and honestly communicating them is the groundwork of sending clear signals. Our lives become richer, more colorful with a greater understanding of ourselves and others.

So how do we learn to become aware of our true needs and wants, and to advocate respectfully for ourselves while honoring the needs and wants of others? The journey of self and other begins by *raising our awareness of body language.*

Connection Two: Becoming Aware of Body Language

Even though Jay and I have been married for almost 18 years, I continue to discover better ways to communicate with him. He enjoys talking to me about changes in law. I confess that I am more interested in other topics; nevertheless, because Jay is an attorney, I understand that he likes to talk about law. Since I love him, I listen.

Occasionally while he is talking, my mind drifts from the subject of law because I do not comprehend his intent, thoughts, and feelings. I have a difficult time understanding the significance of the words and the emotions behind them.

Using some of the skills of reading body language that are explained in this chapter, I look at his entire face and body posture. Listening to his voice, I notice that it is flat, lacking inflection, and that the words are mostly factual. His body language is not communicating effectively how he is *feeling* about the topic. His intents, thoughts and feelings are not sending a clear message. Therefore, it is a challenge for me to read his signals and understand the content and *significance* of his communication.

I ask, "Can you explain, using words that express how you feel, so that I can understand you better?"

His facial expression changes, his shoulders tense, his forehead is more furled at the center and his eyes look a little narrower when he explains, "I'm somewhat worried about how the new estate law may affect future cases."

Now, I understand the significance of our conversation and can listen better, because his communication and body signals correspond with an emotional state of … "somewhat worried."

Nonverbal communication or "body language" is the process of sending and receiving wordless messages by means of hand and finger gestures, body postures, facial expressions and emotional tones of voice. Also included are grooming habits, body positioning in space and consumer-product designs (e.g., clothing signals, fast-food tastes, artificial colors and flavors, engineered fragrances, video images and computer-graphic displays). In short, nonverbal cues include all the signs and signals – audio, visual, tactile and chemical – used by human beings to express themselves apart from manual languages and speech (Givens, 2004, electronic flyer, American Anthropological Association, Center for Nonverbal Studies). Messages sent through our signs and signals communicate more than just the words alone.

Me, Too?

Casual conversations and unspoken social rules are confusing to people on the autism spectrum. For example, I never knew for certain if I was included in a group unless I directly asked. I had difficulty joining up with a group of my peers who were casually chatting. By the time I thought of a bit of information to add or a question to ask, the topic had shifted. Also, I preferred to stand outside the perimeter, where I would be less likely to be crowded and bumped. Classmates over-talked one another, interrupting and changing subjects, using clever nicknames and codes. Often communication happened through eye signals rather than words. I could observe the exchange but was unable to decipher or find it meaningful.

An example of this was when I was a junior in high school and my friend Nancy suggested:

"Let's go over to the Mileage (a short-order café and gas station across from our school) for coke and fries!" As everyone turned to leave, I asked, "Me, too?"

"Of, course, you too! You don't have to ask *every* time," Nancy added as she linked arms with me guiding me down the stairs and out the front door of the school. I tolerated her touch, not wanting to be difficult. I did not read her friendliness as a signal that I am to be *included … every time.*

In situations like this, I felt that I was way on the outside looking in. It seemed to me that everyone else understood the unspoken language of group consensus, as I have later learned – heads and shoulders leaning toward one another, arms touching, eye-to-eye contact and, in this situation, wide smiles all around at the prospect of listening to rock-and-roll music, drinking cokes, eating fries and possibly flirting with one of the college guys who hung out at the café.

Emotions

Our emotions are signals telling us how to interpret the way things are. We are sending our perceptions through our emotional states. Our emotions, then, determine our body language. Happiness, sadness, joy, anger, frustration, all of our emotions, are revealed through our body language. When another person reads our emotional signals and responds, we can communicate with one another. We learn to see the way things are, including another person's point of view, which may be different from our own.

Mental States of Others

Individuals on the autism spectrum are often challenged by not having effective systems for interpreting social signals. Thus, "numerous studies have investigated the degree to which children with autism have difficulty attributing mental states – such as intents, thoughts, and feelings – to themselves and others in order to understand social behavior" (Quill, 2000, p. 5). As a result, these children may not understand when their classmates say one thing but mean another. For example, if a child is uncoordinated and a bully wants to get a cheap laugh at the swimming pool, he or she may say in a false-friendly tone of voice, "Let's get Sally to jump first, she is a way-cool swimmer." Eager to please and be liked, Sally believes the statement and jumps into the deep end of the pool even though she is not able to swim.

Moving in Harmony

Even the way we move sends signals that cause others to form opinions about us. Thus, "it's not just what you say or how much you speak. It's also how you move. Your body language plays a role in how likeable you appear to strangers" (Demarais & White, 2004, p. 133).

Day after day millions of passengers are observed by security guards in airports across the country and around the world. Observers are trained to notice people who stand out or look suspicious. Nervous gestures, an unusual style of dressing, eye movement and suspicious behavior are noted. Apparently, I stood out, because I was frisked and scanned each time I passed the scanner. When I asked why I was always checked, the security person frisking me responded that she did not know, dismissing it as probably "just random checking."

Serendipitously, I discovered one day when I caught a glimpse of myself in a one-way mirror that the way I moved and held my body was sending a message of tense and "nervous." I saw the stiffness in my demeanor *before* I recognized my own reflection and *filtered* what I saw, transforming it into my self-made image of *how I look*.

Based on this new self-awareness, on my next trip I modeled my body language after the other passengers . . . I let the tension go in my neck and dropped my shoulders, smiled a little, casually removed my shoes, placing them with my bag into the gray plastic tub, looked around at others – but not too much. Then I placed the tray on the track, glanced at the next gentleman in line and walked at the same speed and gait as the other travelers. Luckily, I did not accidentally brush or touch the walls of the kiosk as I walked through. Success! My body movement blended with the others, and I avoided the uncomfortable experience of a security scan.

Reading Faces

People on the spectrum of autism have learned to interpret signs and symbols as they relate to objects, not people. For instance, we can easily find Elmo in a maze because we focus on objects rather than the social situation in the picture. However, we can learn to read faces and decipher body language, and as we do this, we can develop new pathways in our brains to create useful processes for sending and receiving clear signals.

Recognizing and understanding facial expressions is a critical component of reading body language. When we are able to read faces, we *resonate to mutual emotions* – one of the bases of communication. Resonating means to echo back the emotional state of someone else, the mirroring and synchronicity of the same behavior. The more a person "feels" the presence of another, the more the two connect – he moves in his chair and she follows, he touches his hair and she touches her hair within a few seconds. It is a subliminal paralleling with or without eye contact.

> One of the main mutual adjustments is in facial expression. When we see a happy face (or an angry one), it evokes the corresponding emotion in us, albeit subtly. To the degree we take on the pace, posture, and facial expression of another person, we start to inhabit their emotional space; as our body mimics the other's, we begin to experience emotional attunement …The extent to which we master this emotional curriculum determines our level of social competence. (Goleman, 1998, p. 137)

Out of Focus

Considering the importance of being able to recognize facial expressions, it is no surprise that communication becomes challenging when you have difficulty in this area. Thus, even with good verbal skills, the ability to initiate and sustain reciprocal conversational flow is reduced because critical information is missing.

Until recently, reading faces was very difficult for me. I could sense facial expression in my body as a nonverbal emotion, but not read – recognize – faces. At first, just as with most deficiencies, I did not know what I did not know, that people glean useful information from facial expression.

When I was a young girl, people's eyes, noses, foreheads, chins and mouths were a blur, I could not separate the various features of a face and store the image in a retrievable way. As a result of seeing parts of the face and not an integrated whole, I looked for anything that moved. Looking directly at eyes caused me to lose myself, my sense of identity, so I stared at mouths. I noticed that when people talked, their mouth moved the most, so I learned to search a face until I could see the moving shape of a mouth. I was using a rudimentary system of interpretation, like a newborn baby searching for a mother's eyes, mouth or breast.

I realized that I could see mouths better if someone wore bright red lipstick. So at church, I searched in purses until I found a shiny tube of Revlon lipstick and attempted to apply it to people's lips regardless of gender.

She Likes Me, She Likes Me Not

Reading faces and facial expression helps you assess a person's character and find clues to what he or she is like and is likely to do.

> *One of the skills of face reading is to recognize how to see when someone's face can provide important clues to his or her personality and behavior and to be able to do this regardless of the person's background.* (Brown, 2000, p. 11)

Mapmaking

Through study and practice, I have learned to read faces and body language by forming a system of interpretation that does not use an actual face as a model. I required a simple icon using geometric shapes that my object-oriented brain could map and retrieve efficiently.

By mapping the face using rectangles and circles, segregating the parts into four basic areas or zones from the top of the head to the bottom of the chin, you will become competent at reading faces (based on Brown, 2000). When you develop clear neural pathways and super highways for instant processing of information about faces, the shapes, geometric patterns, will become second nature.

There are five basic face shapes – oval, round, square, triangle and inverted triangle.

Mapping the Zones of a Face

Zone One: **hairline** to the top of the **eyebrows**

Zone Two: **eyebrows** to the bottom of the **eyes**

Zone Three: **nose** and **cheekbones**

Zone Four: **mouth** to the top of the **chin**

Just as we use roadmaps to find our way in unfamiliar territory, the face icon is a mental template that you can superimpose over your own face and other faces to create a roadmap. The geometric shapes give us points of reference, landmarks for our brains to use in creating new pathways.

Six Face Puzzle Pieces

forehead

eyes

nose

cheeks

mouth

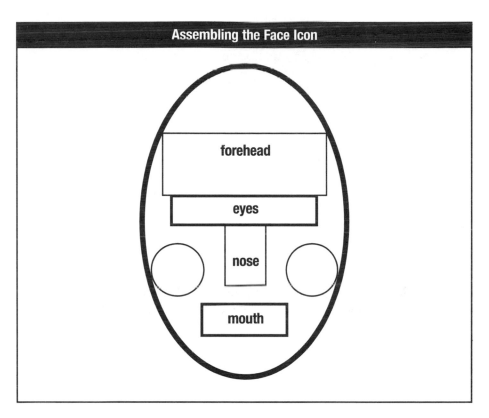

Memorize this face icon. Now, look at your own face in the mirror as you remember the shapes. Visualize them as an overlay or transparency. Mentally adapt the puzzle shapes to fit over your own the face. Go back to the loose puzzle shapes and memorize them. One suggestion for learning the shapes is to number the puzzle pieces if you are good at numbering systems or to invent a interesting story. I think of R2 D2, the loveable robot in *Star Trek*, to help me remember the shapes. This is how I practice.

A Bag on My Head?

Look into a mirror. Really look, to actually see your own face. Often we do not truly look at our own face. Observe without judgment or comparison. Wear lightly tinted sunglasses if it is impossible for you to look directly into your eyes. (It is sometimes helpful to use a headband to hold your hair off your forehead and to drape a solid-colored towel over your shoulders so you can concentrate on your face. I discovered that I could be impartial if I placed a grocery bag over my head in which I had cut out an oval shape the size of my face. Fold the extra paper behind your head and tape it to keep the bag in place.) Look into the mirror until you see the rectangle shape over your eyes. Observe the outline of a rectangle, see proportions not details.

Eyes: Visualize a horizontal rectangle.
Where are your eyes in relation to the rest of your face?
In the middle or are they higher?
Are they close together or widely set?
Look into a mirror until you note the proportions.
What shape are your eyebrows?
Are they full and bushy, thin and straight?

Nose: Is your nose longer than square, or shorter? Is it wide at the base or straight? Can you see your nostrils, or are they hidden?

Mouth: What shape is your mouth? Are your lips thin or full?

Chin: What shape is your chin – oval, round, square or pointed?

Forehead: What shape is your forehead? Is it long or short, wide or narrow?

Hairline: Is your hairline straight, curved? What is the texture of your hair – curly, straight, thick or thin?

Ears: Notice where your ears are placed; are they high or low in relation to your eyes? Large or small? Flat or sticking out? What length are your ear lobes? (0.4 inch from the point where the ear joins the skin is considered average.)

What did you discover about your face? Notice the difference between the left and right sides. Is one side more developed than the other? The right side is considered creative and the left logical. If the right side is more fully defined, it may indicate that you process visually, using pictures more than words, and that you are creative. If the left side is more developed, then you probably are more logical and analytical, excelling in math or science. If you are interested in learning more about what this information means in terms of body language, read *The Nonverbal Dictionary of Gestures, Signs & Body Cues* (Givens, 2002).

Reading the Body

The information learned about reading a face can also be applied to your body. In the following, we will use a body icon to separate the body into zones that will help your brain map the different areas of the body. Learning to observe and raise your awareness is the first step. Just as we did for the face, geometric shapes of ovals, rectangles and a square are assembled into a useful body icon that is stored as an object in the brain to be retrieved efficiently as "body shape."

Reading body language is like looking at a still photograph and then seeing a video of the same picture. As you practice developing pathways in your brain, you may be surprised to discover the amount of useful information about body language that you will be able to process. What was once a blurry image becomes an integral unit. The icon becomes a useful tool for processing the myriad bits of data that we encounter daily.

Interpreting Moods

Knowing how to read body language helps us in determining the mood of another person and assists us in knowing how and when to trust others. For example, are they interested, hostile, friendly or seductive by the way they hold their bodies?

Begin to notice body language as you walk in the street, wait for a bus or sit in a reception room. One caution about doing this exercise, *do not stare directly at people*. In U.S. culture, this is considered impolite, rude, intrusive, and may even be seen as a threat. Other societies have slightly different tolerances for staring. Be as discrete as an anthropologist as you study to observe without influencing change. Try to blend in with others by paralleling them, doing the same thing. Order a cup of coffee and sit at a corner table or near a window. Read a magazine or book – the objective is to look natural and unobtrusive.

For now, *simply observe* without making interpretations; notice without judgment. Gather images. This is like an athlete observing star players – watching the style and form of delivery – before applying any improvements to your technique. The following are some suggestions for what to observe. As you practice, add them to your mental list.

How does the person hold his shoulders?
Is her head held upright or leaning forward?
Is the person alert, smiling, or talking?
Are the movements fast or slow?
What are the person's gestures? Directed toward self or others?

As you answer these questions, you will form new pathways in your neural brain circuit, building reference points to categorize information about people. You will become more adept at seeing body shapes and body language.

As you discretely observe someone or look at your own body in a full-length mirror, visually divide the body into four major zones. The separated areas will help you focus by creating new pathways in your brain.

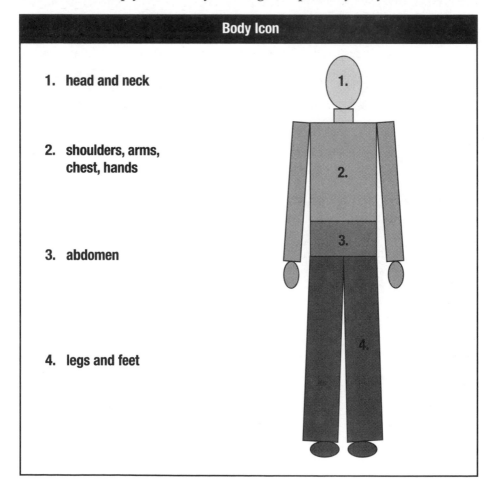

Body Icon

1. **head and neck**

2. **shoulders, arms, chest, hands**

3. **abdomen**

4. **legs and feet**

Connection Three: Defining Our Needs and Wants

The benefit of learning to read faces and body language is that I can understand what other people expect from me. I can decode body signals, ask for what I want, including advocating for myself. If we do not send clear signals that others can easily read, we do not fit into the culture and are often dismissed as odd, stiff – off in our own world – when, in fact, it is the system of signals that is inconsistent. If we do not send information that is easily interpreted, others assign a meaning, an interpretation, to our body language, and it may not be the message we intend!

Meeting your needs, finding someone with whom you can share your interests, being creative and expressing yourself through art, music, math, auto mechanics or science, depends upon revealing your emotions. Learning to communicate our emotions and understanding signs, symbols and behaviors determines how happy we can ultimately be.

Unless we are willing to examine and change the messages we are sending and receiving, we will stay the way we are. Of course, if you are happy with the way you are, satisfied with your communication style and the way you are perceived by others, then you do not need to change. Skip to Liane Willey's chapter, "Disclosure and Self-Advocacy: An Open Door Policy," to learn about fun and active ways to tell others about autism spectrum disorders and stand up for yourself. You will relate to her outgoing style.

As for me, the introvert, I knew that if I did not change after my divorce, I would likely make the same choices and choose a similar, limiting relationship again. I decided to do whatever it took to change. That was 20 years ago, and, despite major strides, I am still growing and learning.

Before my divorce I depended upon others to decide how I felt, what choices I made and what I needed. I was a people pleaser! I took helpful comments as criticism and judged myself for any perceived deficiencies. The difference between then and now is that I welcome nonjudgmental feedback and have learned to love and accept myself. Roger Meyer mentions the importance of self-acceptance in his chapter, "Being Your Own Case Manager."

Using the skills discussed in Connections One and Two, in this section, we will journey inward to find our authentic true selves.

Mask as Self

Mass advertisers would have us believe that our self-identity is defined by the job we have, the kind of vehicle we drive, our outward appearance and the status of our friends. The mental image we construct is the mask we wear to present an idea of a "self" to the world. After a time we come to believe that this mask is our authentic self.

> ...*When you don't know who you are, you create a mind-made self as a substitute for your beautiful divine being and cling to that fearful and needy self. Protecting and enhancing that false sense of self then becomes your primary force...When you know who you truly are, there is an abiding sense of peace. You could call it joy because that's what joy is: vibrantly alive peace. It is the joy of knowing yourself as the very life essence before life takes on form. That is the joy of Being – of being who you truly are. (Tolle, 2003, p. 52, 57)*

Journey Inward

I believe that the path to one's "true" self can be found in silence and meditation. When our world is quiet, we can discover who we are and what we truly need and desire. The habit of our mind is to stay active, repeating the "image" that we have created of who we are. It is an illusion that our mind defends by denying our *true* needs and desires. It is as if we keep the message level set on high to drown out information that is inconsistent, just like when teenagers put their fingers in their ears to avoid hearing a parent while humming loudly.

> *When most of us tune in to the mind, listening to what passes through, we become aware of an insistent internal conversation with ourselves. The inner dialogue is the endless stream of thinking that comments on our experiences. We are often more tuned in to its commentary than we are to what's actually happening, with the result that we miss the moment. (Borysenko, 1987, p. 35)*

As we learn how to calm our active, thinking mind, we can observe our emotions and feelings in our bodies and find our authentic or true self in the *space* between our breaths. To accomplish this, observe your breathing without changing its rhythm. Breathe in and out while noticing your feelings, staying present in the moment. Name the feelings – my anger, my joy, my sadness – and let the feeling go as you exhale.

When we pause to observe "how" we are breathing, we bring awareness. In the pause between breaths, notice the sounds of your environment without judging. During this quiet space, we can begin to discover our true selves.

Inhale-Exhale

(Allow 10 minutes for this exercise at first and increase over time, to one hour)

1. Find a quiet place and a comfortable chair; place your feet on the floor.

2. Notice your breath without changing it.

3. As you inhale, say silently, "my inhalation," and as you exhale, say "my exhalation." Just breathe.

4. Notice your breath. Is it cool or hot, fast or slow?

5. Practice breathing like this for 5 minutes.

As you become familiar with the sensations that arise in your body, try to mentally identify the emotion. Say to yourself, "my anger," "my joy," "my sadness," without clinging to the story behind the emotion. Inhale and notice, and as you exhale, let the emotion go, as if you were dropping a beach ball into a mountain stream. The next inhalation may bring a similar or a different emotion; again notice, name the emotion and breathe out the emotion with the exhalation, letting go completely of any residual feelings.

Over time, the constant thinking, planning and ruminating will cease. As you feel comfortable with the process of finding your true self, you can increase the time for this activity; 45 minutes to an hour is good amount of time to meditate daily. You will benefit from practicing breath awareness each day for the rest of your life. Choose a time of day that will be consistent, so your mind can look forward to a predictable quiet time each day. If you feel overwhelmed with intense feelings or too many emotions on a regular basis, please seek assistance from a mental health professional.

Becoming Aware of Your Emotions

I become aware of my emotions each moment by noticing where they are located in my body. For me, emotions have temperatures and frequencies. Others may have a completely different way of experiencing emotion. For some, emotions are hot, cool, or have sound or texture. My emotions are the vibration and frequency of colors. Joy is pink and warm, happy is golden yellow and hot, and sad is blue-gray and cool.

The first time I discovered a feeling in my body that was an emotion was when I was 4 years old and sitting in the front row of my Sunday school class. Mrs. Prunty, our teacher, is standing at the front of the room singing a welcome song. The song has become my favorite. "Climb, climb up sunshine mountain faces all aglow." Morning sunlight is radiating through the stained-glass window, forming a rainbow of light that cascades over the braids wrapped tightly around Mrs. Prunty's head. I feel warmth from the sunshine in my arms. Happiness and joy are the emotion. Sunlight is paired with emotion. Sunlight is love. Wishing to recreate the pleasant feeling in my arms from the nursery-class experience, I now hold prisms in the sunlight making rainbows of joy.

I have found other emotions while listening to music and, later, while playing the violin. The vibration and resonance of the A string make my arms feel warm like sunshine. The D string is sadness and the lowest string, G, reflects grief. The highest, E, string is excitement and euphoria; violet purple. It is a cool breeze on a hot summer evening.

Each time I see a rainbow, I feel love and joy. Each time I play my violin, I feel love and joy through the vibration. After many years of sitting in Zen meditation, I have learned to transfer the emotions I feel with light and music to the people who are significant in my life.

Accepting Your Mistakes

Learning to accept ourselves with all of our faults, needs and desires is the beginning of acceptance. We can forgive ourselves for the times when we have been harmful or negative. We are human; we all make mistakes. It is how we respond to these circumstances that determines how fully we can discover and become our authentic selves.

As a teenager, I wanted to be perfect. With a fragile ego, I needed to maintain a certain Vogue-fashion image of myself in order to feel worthwhile. I endeavored to create an impeccable mental image of a fashion model. When I made a mistake, I tried even harder to be perfect. I berated myself many times each day for my imperfections. No one could criticize me more than I did. I kept others at a distance, fearing disclosure of the fraud I suspected I was.

When we become aware of our imperfections and begin to accept them as part of ourselves, we are at the beginning of *becoming who we really are*. Dropping the old image of ourselves can be traumatic, however. "What if I don't like myself?" "What if no one will love or even like the authentic, messy, imperfect me?" We learn to be kind to ourselves, to treat ourselves gently, cherishing ourselves when we make a mistake, loving ourselves as a parent cares for a child. I love my baby grandson no matter what he does, accepting spit-up and dirty diapers, along with his smiles and coos, as adorable Patrick.

Compassion

In the process of observing yourself, allow for a time of discomfort and change. We gradually transform our habitual, knee-jerk responses to people and events in our lives. We begin to notice when we feel genuinely happy, peaceful and loving. As a result, when anger and rage appear spontaneously, we can choose our response to it, and not react with the old pattern and pathway in our brain.

Recently I ran out of paper in the middle of a writing project and had to go to the store to buy more. As I stood in line at Office Max waiting to check out, I *chose* to feel annoyed and then angry, when a woman with three small children cut in ahead of me.

The intensity of my anger surprised me. Standing there waiting, I became curious about an apparent need that I had to hold my place against line crashers. I took a deep breath and felt the anger rising from my throat into my cheeks. Then, as I turned to look directly into the woman's face, ready to "politely" show her where the end of the line was, my anger dramatically shifted to empathy.

Upon truly *seeing* her tired-looking face, I smiled in self-recognition. My angry emotion dissolved as I remembered my own daughters when they were about her children's ages, the stress of managing work and home, parenting, responsibilities of money, and how quickly the years have passed. She returned my smile and gently ruffled her smallest child's hair as she waited for her change. I *chose* to respond with kindness instead of reacting out of habit. As she picked up her package, she turned and nodded thanks to me. I smiled back, grateful for the experience and the opportunity to change.

This scenario could have turned out differently if I had responded by acting annoyed. Beyond the episode in the store, the stress of my anger could have stayed with me long after the event and might have affected the rest of my day – possibly also her day and her children's day.

The way we respond to the events in our lives can reinforce negative habit patterns or can form other more desired neural pathways in our brains. If we berate ourselves when we do badly, then that is the neural pathway for shame that becomes well formed. If, on the other hand, we can see the humor or have compassion in a situation – seeing it as it is, not as we imagine it to be – we can develop pathways that allow us to be happy, loving and kind to others and to ourselves.

Positive emotions – love, joy, happiness – allow our bodies to stay healthy. This does not mean that we go around blissfully happy all the time. Rather, we express our emotions as they occur in a respectful way. The way we express our feelings shapes our lives. We can communicate by making better connections when we improve our emotional intelligence, our EQ. In *The Emotional Revolution* (2002), Norman Rosenthal speaks of emotion providing us with a special kind of intelligence. One part of our brain's memory system seems to record facts and events, whereas the other records emotional experiences.

> *While intelligence has traditionally been considered a purely intellectual function, the concept of emotional intelligence is gaining ground. In both personal and professional life, we now know, success depends to some extent on understanding what feelings can and cannot do to make us healthier or less healthy, to promote recovery or induce death. (Rosenthal, 2002, p. 5)*

The differences in symbols, signs and behavior that cause miscommunication between those on the spectrum of autism and others could be reduced dramatically if everyone increased their emotional intelligence. There would be excellence in relationships, the workplace, schools and community. We would encourage and support diversity. There would be fewer suicides and murders.

Keeping Boundaries

Defining our personal space and the boundaries that we need to feel safe is triggered by the emotions we feel in our bodies. A visual image of boundary setting is a picket fence. Usually, there is a gate somewhere in the fence that has a latch or some other closing mechanism. You can come and go, and the fence keeps pets in and unwanted intruders out. People generally respect a yard with a fence and a gate.

This metaphor can be applied to our life. If we have an understanding of how our emotions feel in our bodies, we can become aware of what makes us happy, sad, energized or weak. We will know when someone is crossing a boundary, because we will feel fear, hurt or anger. Each time we recognize one of these emotions, we can place a "mental" picket in our personal boundary fence. We can tell someone, "When you ignored me yesterday at lunch, I felt hurt." When we learn to process our emotions before they become stuck or buried, we become more confident that we can take care of ourselves when we reveal our diagnosis.

When we understand our feelings and emotions, we can ask for our needs to be met. If we do not understand our emotions, how can we know what we need and be clear about what to ask? How can we ask but not demand that our needs and wants be met?

One of the first self-help books I read after my divorce was *Prescriptions for Happiness* by K. Keyes (n.d.). Among other helpful messages I learned, the following has stayed with me: "Just simply ask for what you want without playing deceptive games, without loading down with separating emotions or implied threats, without using a heavy tone of voice. Simply but definitely ask for what you want!" (p. 21). You may not get what you want, and that is OK. The important thing is to *ask in a kind voice without demanding it.*

First prescription:

> Ask for what you want but don't demand it.
>
> Use liberally as needed.

Second prescription:

> Accept whatever happens for now.
>
> Memorize this prescription so that you'll always have it. Use whenever you need it.

Third prescription:

R℞ Turn up your love even if you don't get what you want.

To be used liberally all of the time. Refills: Every heart has an infinite supply whether it's used or not.

From Keyes, K. (n.d.). *Prescriptions for happiness.* St. Mary, KY: Living Love Publications. Reprinted with permission.

By following these three prescriptions, we will develop relationships that are based upon honesty and trust. We can ask for our needs to be met and accept, for now, what happens. "Be content with more or less, rather than all or none" (Keyes, n.d., p. 113).

Trust

Many of us have been abused and neglected, have histories of broken promises and lost trust. As a result, we are suspicious of others and their motives. Learning to trust begins with ourselves. How many times have we promised ourselves something only to break our promise? When we take our commitments to ourselves seriously, we begin to notice how it feels to have our needs and wants honored. If I push through something challenging or difficult, such as writing this chapter, I often make a promise to myself that I honor. I like to smell fresh flowers, browse in a bookstore or go to a movie. If I keep my promise to myself, I value the longing of my inner child who wants to play and not work so hard.

When we value our self-worth, we project a different image of selves to others, our body language communicates a message that *we can be trusted.* Since in the law of nature like attracts like, we also attract others who are more likely to be trustworthy.

Some of the attributes of a person we can trust are: honest, open, steadfast, candid, ethical, and moral. A caution is in order here: sometimes a person we thought could be trusted insincerely displays many of these attributes. We discover, perhaps painfully, that he or she has a hidden dark side.

A friend, Jennifer, wrote a dissertation after observing the social interactions of individuals in our social group for people on the spectrum of autism, the Get-Together. She observed that many people reported being bullied at work and had a history of being teased as children. She attributed this vulnerability in part to being unaware of a front- and back-stage performance in people's behaviors and communications. That is, that people have one behavior on the front stage where others are observing them and another quite different behavior back of the stage, behind the curtain. We will take a closer look at these dual behaviors in the next section.

Connection Four: Dancing the Communication Dance

How can we advocate effectively for ourselves and reveal a diagnosis if we are unaware of our emotions? How can we connect and communicate effectively with others and set boundaries unless we know what we need and want?

When we give up our automatic, often negative inner voice, we learn to accept our mistakes, set boundaries, and honor our needs in relation to others. We must trust the true self, the inner voice, to help us decide what to reveal about ourselves.

Behind the Curtain

Now that we have learned about how to develop trust by honoring and trusting ourselves, and how to ask for our needs and wants to be met, we discover that there are multiple layers of communication that are *not immediately apparent* – that people may say one thing but do another. This realization takes on particular significance as we put together everything we have talked about so far in preparation for the ultimate act of self-awareness, trust and effective communication: *self-disclosure.*

Public versus back stage is a concept described by Erving Goffman in *The Presentation of Self in Everyday Life* (1959). Using the metaphor of a theatrical performance to give us insight into how people live with and relate to one another, Goffman proposes that there are multiple layers to most situations, including a front (region) and back stage (region), with the outermost region – the one we see – not necessarily the controlling one. There are multiple productions going on simultaneously, and the actors are saying one thing on the front stage and doing another on the back.

Discovering that people have public- and back-stage selves is quite revealing, especially to those of us on the autism spectrum for whom deciphering "hidden" communication and subtle social behaviors is not automatic. With effort we learn that the actors (other people) behave with decorum and good taste in front of an audience, but back stage, these same actors often seem different and "out of character." The back stage is where we can expect no members of the audience to be.

In her doctoral dissertation, *Embracing Differences*, Jennifer Babiracki (2002) writes,

> *When performances move to the backstage away from the audience's view, individuals tend to do and say things they typically would not say or do in the front stage in front of an audience. Within the front stage, individuals are visible to their audience, which in turn influence their choice of behavior. (pp. 42-43)*

Sorting out personal/private information from public information is complex. Using a visual model helps. In this exercise, we are using a pie-shaped model. Think of yourself playing softball with you up to bat. As you look out into the field, imagine that the players are like people in your daily life. Some are close and some are distant. The ball is pitched and you swing, hitting the ball and watching to see where it is likely to go.

Think of the baseball in this example as information about yourself that you share with others. *What you tell* and *whom you tell* is determined by how intimate and/or distant people are in your life. It is not just the physical distance; it is *emotional* distance as well.

Our real world is not a softball diamond with a home plate and a catcher behind us. Other people *surround* us. When you become comfortable with the concept of degrees of self-disclosure, you can visually surround yourself with pie-shaped wedges with you in the center of a hexagon.

Inch or Mile ... Degrees of Self-Disclosure

There are degrees of self-disclosure with many uncertain or gray areas. A gray area is where we may need to ask for help in deciding whom to tell what and when to tell. We can reveal parts or all of the information, depending on how well we know someone. For an example, Betty, the check-out clerk at Lund's grocery store, sees me frequently, but we are not personal friends. At times, she may have to repeat things to me because of my problem of deciphering sounds in a noisy environment. I say, "Sorry, I have trouble hearing in a noisy area" – I don't tell her about my diagnosis of autism. Frequently, other shoppers have trouble hearing too, so she understands. I prefer to disclose using small steps, an inch – not a mile – of information about myself.

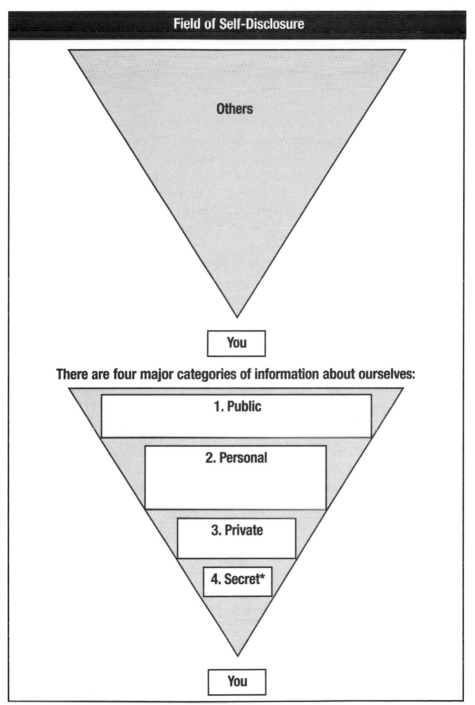

Field of Self-Disclosure

Others

You

There are four major categories of information about ourselves:

1. Public

2. Personal

3. Private

4. Secret*

You

* A secret may need to be disclosed, if it is illegal, dangerous or vital to your health. Example: A man with diabetes told me his secret because his life depended upon getting immediate help.

I assess the situation to see if telling part or all about autism will be beneficial or detrimental. Often I explain things from my personality type, introvert, or a physical need I may have, "Let's not to sit under a fluorescent light because the flicker interferes with my brain waves and gives me a headache." Or, "Action movies are too loud or violent; horror films, scary. Can we choose something else?" At other times, I tell people that I have been diagnosed with autism. Usually this information is shared in conjunction with volunteering as a speaker for autism. In those situations, it quite naturally follows to be straightforward and tell people.

In working with others on the autism spectrum, and for my own use, it occurred to me that since many of us process information better visually, a worksheet might be helpful for evaluating the pros and cons of self-disclosure.

- On a scale of 1-10 ask, yourself how important it is to make a decision about your situation. If you choose "3" or higher (with "1" being not important at all and "10" being extremely important), use the worksheet. Level 1 or 2 can probably be resolved by talking to a friend.

- If you are wondering who to ask when you need help, review the following description:

Helpful people are people who:

1. You know you **can trust**

2. Who know you well and have **your best interests** in mind

3. Can **keep a confidence** and not gossip

Ultimately, you are the one to decide when it is safe to tell someone, and who to trust.

In Chapter 2, Kassiane Sibley describes six steps to self-advocacy and disclosure that are very helpful. Also, as both she and later Liane Willey (Chapter 6) suggest, you can use letter writing as a tool rather than telling a person, depending on your personal comfort level and situation.

Disclosure Worksheet	
1-10 Level _____ Situation:	
☐ Tell	☐ Not Tell
Possible result:	Possible result:
☐ Tell Later	☐ Need Help
Possible result:	☐ Get Help: Name: _____ Phone: _____ Email: _____ Notes:

Disclosure Worksheet

1-10 Level ___8___

Situation: My supervisor wants me to move to a different cubicle. It will be noisy and distracting in the new location.

☐ Tell	☐ Not Tell
- that I am easily distracted. - sensitive and on the spectrum of autism	- just move and make the best of it
Possible result:	Possible result:
She may pass me over for a promotion next month.	be miserable, may make mistakes, less work from distractions

☐ Tell Later	☒ Need Help
- Try it for a week - Say: I'll give it a try, but it may be too noisy for the kind of work I do.	- Should I disclose about my autism? - If I do what should I say? ☒ Get Help: Name: Mary Phone: 000-000-0000 Email: mary@friend.org
Possible result:	Notes: Mary suggests to try the new cubicle for one week – call her if I need more help.
A week may be too hard. I may be short tempered.	

To Tell

Tell if the information will be:
- helpful for your relationship
- important for safety
- essential at work

Ask yourself the five "w" questions and one "h" question:
who, what, when, where and *why*, and *how*

Who do I tell? _____

What do I say? _____

When do I tell? _____

Where do I tell? _____

Why would I tell? _____

How do I tell?_____

I tell if I am having an "autistic" day; that is, when my autism is causing me to be hypersensitive and processing auditory information is challenging. If it is a stranger, I tell only what is necessary. "Sorry, too noisy for me." When I know a person fairly well and the music is too loud, I say, "Could we turn down the volume? With my autism, I can process conversation better without the loud music." Practice several different ways of asking for your needs to be met so that when the situation arises, you can easily ask without sounding irritated or demanding.

Sometimes I tell to educate and desensitize an issue. For example, I may appear rude when someone interrupts me. "I'm sorry, I was lost in thought and didn't hear you." See what feels best for you.

Not Tell

Several years ago I applied to volunteer as a healer and teacher at a health crisis center and wondered if I should tell the director about my autism at the interview. I discussed this with my husband and a close friend. We reviewed all of the possible scenarios and decided together that, for now, not telling would be fine, that I could meet the required expectations and adapt when necessary.

Tell Later

After I had volunteered successfully at the health crisis center for several years, I decided to run for a board position for the Autism Society of America. I asked Howard, the director of the center, if he felt comfortable giving me a personal reference.

He said, "Yes, I would be happy to." Then he asked, "What is your interest in autism?"

I took this natural opportunity to tell him about the dramatic increase in the incidence of autism we are facing, and that I was diagnosed in 1995 with high-functioning autism.

He responded, "I'm surprised. I never would have known if you hadn't told me."

By then, we had developed a friendly rapport and he trusted me, so I felt free to disclose about my diagnosis.

Sometimes telling others about a diagnosis of autism can help promote better communication and understanding. On the other hand, it can also be detrimental. When to tell and when not to tell others ... this is the dilemma. I suggest that you use the worksheet on page 25 to become clear about the situation so you can ask for help, decide when to tell, or not to tell.

Sometimes telling a supervisor at school or work can prevent a promotion or appointment for leadership. It is important for you to determine by yourself, or with the help of someone you trust, whether a situation you put yourself in would be dangerous. You, ultimately, are responsible for keeping your own self, and others who may be affected, safe.

Liane Holliday Willy, a famous person with Asperger Syndrome and a friend (also author of Chapter 6), wrote *Pretending to Be Normal* (1999). I highly recommend this book, especially the section on "Explaining Who You Are to Those Who Care." For example, I agree with Liane's statement:

> *Debate rages among those in the Asperger's community whether or not people with AS should tell the world about their challenges and idiosyncrasies. Those who choose to keep their AS private can often find creative ways to work through the social norms and educational systems that surround their lives. But for many, particularly those who*

are profoundly affected, it might be more effective to educate others about the disorder both in general terms and as it applies to their own situation. (p. 123)

Exceptions

I have purposely left areas shaded around the rectangular shapes on page 23, because usually there are few clear and simple answers in life. In self-disclosure, many situations are possible. For example, when we have a medical emergency or a health concern, we may tell a casual acquaintance, or even a complete stranger, personal or private information in order to get medical help.

Accidents or injury are also times when you may disclose private information to a police officer or medical assistant without hesitation. When I was in a car accident a few years ago, I told a police officer that I am autistic and have to wear dark polarized sunglasses because I am very sensitive to light. He asked me personal questions, where I lived, where I was going, my age, to determine my mental and physical state, and to see if I needed an ambulance, or if I could drive my damaged car after the accident. He agreed to let me sit on the curb until I felt calm enough to drive my car to the garage.

Disclosure at Work

School and employment are complex areas. Telling schoolmates and coworkers about your diagnosis can be risky. In a competitive place like work, unfortunately, there may be self-centered people who relish knowing information that they can use at an opportune time to better themselves or put you down. These are folks you will place in the Do Not Tell category. Sometimes it is best not to tell. I tend to tell about my autism when the information is essential for safety, or I tell someone in authority. This is a person I trust, who will know how to be helpful. He or she will do or say the right thing and not make a situation worse.

Teasing at work can be very problematic since the bully is often someone who uses covert, passive-aggressive behavior to set someone up to be embarrassed, or discredited. I experienced this on a job when several coworkers resented the way I led my team and purposely withheld information about scheduled meetings and new procedures that needed to be followed.

Fitting In

Humans have a basic survival need to fit in and be accepted. How well we fit in socially is largely determined by how effectively we send and receive communication signs and signals. In a practical book on learning to read and send relationship signals, *Will I Ever Fit In?*, authors Nowicki and Duke (2002) state in their introduction: "Problems in human relationships depend far less upon problems in verbal communication than they depend upon problems in nonverbal communication." On page 14, they go on to say, "Not only are we less aware of what we are communicating nonverbally than we are of the words we are speaking, but our nonverbal communications are also *more continuous.*"

We communicate from birth until death. Learning to send and receive signals and communicate effectively is the central theme of *Ask and Tell.*

Final Steps

In this chapter, we have learned that we have to wake up and become aware, gather information through nonjudgmental observation, to meditate and calm our busy thinking so we can discover our true self ... in the quiet space between our breaths. Then, we discovered how to ask and tell about our diagnosis using the icons and a worksheet, and how to trust ourselves and others.

The final step in the dance is finding happiness and joy by living a *full and rewarding life*. The communication dance is like the swing dance. In swing, you and a partner move back and forth, turning and spinning, momentum changing as you lean in and out, giving and taking, respectfully, joyfully dancing.

Ruth Elaine Joyner Hane *lives with her husband, Jay, in Minneapolis. Their lives are enriched by four grown children, a daughter-in-law, son-in-law, two baby grandsons, three cats and many goldfish. Ruth Elaine is midwest director for the Autism Society of America's board of directors and serves on various ASA committees.*

In addition to consulting with individuals who are challenged with health and well-being, she leads Serenity Circles for developing emotional intelligence, presents workshops on Chi Energy, Avoiding Burnout in the Age of Anxiety, Finding Joy at the Holidays, and Energy Boundaries. Ruth Elaine coaches people within the spectrum of autism and facilitates two social groups. She is a contributing author to Sharing Our Wisdom, *a collection of public presentations.*

A Rubella baby, she received a correct diagnosis of autism in 1995. Defying a prediction of mental retardation in grade school, she graduated Phi Beta Kappa, magna cum laude with a B.S. in human ecology. Presently she is a Reiki master/healer.

References

Babiracki, J. (2002). *Embracing difference.* Unpublished doctoral dissertation, University of St. Thomas.

The Book Laboratory, Inc. (2001). *The little book of Zen.* New York: Barnes & Noble.

Borysenko, J. (1987). *Minding the body, mending the mind.* Reading, MA: A Bantam Book, published by Addison-Wesley Publishing Company.

Brown, S. (2000). *The practical art of face reading.* New York: A Sterling Publishing Co., Inc.

Demarais, A., & White, V. (2004). *First impressions.* New York: Bantam Books, Random House.

Gillingham G., & McClennen, S. (2003). *Sharing our wisdom.* Edmonton, Alt, Canada: Tacit Publishing Inc.

Givens, D. (1983). *Love signals.* New York: Pinnacle Books, Inc. (out of print).

Givens, D. (2002). *The nonverbal dictionary of gestures, signs & body cues.* Spokane, WA: Center for Nonverbal Studies Press.

Givens, D. (2004). Internet posting, Center for Nonverbal Learning. http://members.aol.com/nonverbal2/

Goffman, E. (1959). *The presentation of self in everyday life.* New York: Anchor Books, Doubleday.

Goleman, D. (1995). *Emotional intelligence.* New York: Bantam Books.

Goleman, D. (1998). *Working with emotional intelligence.* New York: Bantam Books.

Holiday Willey, L. (1999). *Pretending to be normal.* London: Jessica Kingsley Publishers.

Jacobs-Stewart, T. (2003). *Paths are made by walking.* New York: Warner Books.

Keyes, K. (n.d.). *Prescriptions for happiness.* St. Mary, KY: Living Love Publications.

Nowicki, S., & Duke, M. (2002). *Will I ever fit in?* New York: Simon & Schuster, Inc.

Quill, K. (2000). *Do watch say listen.* Baltimore: Paul H. Brooks Publishing.

Tolle, E. (2003). *Stillness speaks.* Novato, CA: New World Library, Vancouver: Namaste Publishing.

Williams, D. (1992). *Nobody nowhere.* New York: Avon Books.

CHAPTER 2

Help Me Help Myself: Teaching and Learning Self-Advocacy

Kassiane Sibley

Self-advocacy is a topic I find extremely important because it is so rarely thought about and discussed. I have had to learn advocacy skills the hard way, and I do not want that for my younger peers. I find myself frustrated by parents and professionals who prefer to strive for "indistinguishable from peers" rather than self-sufficiency. Independence does not and should not have to equal typicality, but in so many people's eyes the two are synonymous. I firmly believe that everyone on the autistic spectrum can and should learn advocacy skills. All the examples in this chapter are either my personal experiences or a hybrid of several other people's experiences; all names have been randomly selected for privacy.

One thing autistics[1] and parents of autistics agree upon is the desire for independence. Many skills are taught in an effort to achieve this

---

[1] I use the terms "autistics," "autistic person," "autie," and "Aspie" rather than the politically correct "person with autism" or "person with Asperger Syndrome." I do this intentionally, because I find that person-first language diminishes a vital part of who I am. You cannot remove autism from me; it is part of my identity. I refer to myself as an autie, Aspie, or autistic, and I use those terms for the culture I belong to as well. It is not done to offend, but to remind the reader that autism is not an appendage. Autism is a way of being.

goal, but one of the most important is consistently neglected. This skill is called self-advocacy.

Self-advocacy is the process by which we get our wants and needs met. If we are to be independent, we have to advocate for ourselves. In spite of this blatant truth, few parents and professionals think to teach advocacy. They do not teach advocacy mainly out of ignorance – it does not occur to them that a person on the spectrum needs to be shown how. But the truth of the matter is that we do not naturally learn how to get our needs met the way typical children do. The six-stage procedure described in this chapter addresses autistic persons' need to be directly taught self-advocacy and disclosure. In the following chapter, Stephen Shore also addresses this need, with particular attention to using the IEP to develop skills in self-advocacy and disclosure.

There are several reasons why autistic people tend to have poor self-advocacy skills. First, we do not learn social patterns well, and self-advocacy is a social process. While most of the neurotypical population learns to ask for things by imitation, autistics need explicit instructions. Well-meaning adults often contribute to the problem in our childhood by doing for us what we should be taught to do for ourselves, resulting in *learned dependence* because we do not practice the techniques of advocacy ourselves. The autistic theory-of-mind difference also contributes to our lack of self-advocacy skills: "I know what I need; therefore, so does everyone else." Sometimes an autistic person is not aware that he or she perceives the world differently and, therefore, feels "whiney" asking for accommodation.

Since self-advocacy is an essential skill and autistics do not learn it naturally, we must make a conscious effort to acquire these skills. An adult can teach another adult or a child, a person can try to teach himself, or two teens or adults can work together to practice advocacy skills. Since it tends to be easier to see options in other people's situations than in one's own, the latter approach usually works well. Therefore, the first five stages of self-advocacy presented here utilize a partner or facilitator. The partner's job at the beginning is to steer the tandem bike, but towards the end of the process, the partner pedals. The facilitator provides support, knowledge, and someone with whom to discuss options and ideas. If the advocate gets stuck, the partner serves as an extra head, an extra brain, to suggest ideas. The partner and the advocate also often practice skills together, and the facilitator can be a filter for any tones of voice or wording that may be misperceived as disrespectful by the target audience.

Following is a six-stage plan for learning or teaching self-advocacy skills. The elements of each step are similar in that they all involve preparation, requesting the need, and followup. Who does what and the techniques learned in each stage vary a bit, but each stage builds on the previous one, and there is no set rate of progress. It is all based on comfort with new skills.

The six stages are as follows.

1. *Planning and Modeling.* The first stage demonstrates, with the autistic person's involvement, how to plan for successful self-advocacy. After being involved in the planning of this stage, the person on the autism spectrum observes the partner in the act of advocating for that person.

2. *Facilitation and Confidence Building.* With more responsibility being given to the autistic person in this stage, the partner now serves more to guide the person through the steps of self-advocacy. Thus, while the autistic person is encouraged to do his or her own advocating, the partner is at the ready to step in if necessary.

3. *Partnering and Letter Writing.* Here the procedure of self-advocacy is split roughly 50-50 between the autistic person and the partner. Budding advocates take the lead, but facilitators still offer strong guidance, particularly in the area of role-playing and suggesting the wording to use when asking for accommodations. The partner also still offers much moral support at the time of the actual advocacy, although ideally the person on the spectrum does most of the talking. At this stage, the autistic person is also introduced to letter writing as part of his or her self-advocacy efforts.

4. *Moral Support.* At this point the partner continues to assist with the preparation for self-advocacy, but the goal is to have the person on the autism spectrum do all the talking, with the partner in the vicinity for emergencies and maintaining self-confidence.

5. *Taking the Lead.* The autistic person leads the way in all aspects of the self-advocacy effort. The partner still assists, but only under the direction of the self-advocate.

6. *Independent Self-Advocacy.* In this cultivating stage, the advocate undertakes all the preparation, presentation, and evaluation in a completely independent manner.

The previous steps are to be used as a general outline rather than hard and fast rules. For example, the same person may be at Stage 3 for one kind of self-advocacy and Stage 4 for another. Additionally, if an advocate slips backwards a stage or two, that is to be viewed as natural, not a source of shame or defeat. For example, an autistic advocate may easily be able to explain his or her needs in the familiar context of a classroom, but may need more guidance and support from a facilitator the first few times he or she is seeking accommodations and understanding at a new job.

Step 1: Planning and Modeling

Ideally the first step starts when children are very young, but many of us will be adults before we think to seek help or to help ourselves. This stage involves planning and modeling. As with all the stages, the first step is to identify what we have to ask for. For myself and many of the kids I know, the problems are usually sensory.

Scenario

Tommy is very light sensitive. His first-grade teacher sees him squint a great deal, so she seats him under a downlight right by the glare from the whiteboard. Not knowing any better, the teacher thinks she is helping by making this change. Even though he is extremely uncomfortable, since Tommy has had no self-advocacy training, he does not know effective ways to ask for change. Instead, he constantly leaves his seat for a dark corner, refuses to look at the front of the room, turns off the lights, and has meltdowns when punished for these actions. Tommy, his teacher, his parents, and his classmates are all very frustrated with the situation.

Self-Advocacy

Sasha is in another first-grade class and has the same kind of visual issues as Tommy. But unlike Tommy, Sasha has a self-advocacy buddy. Meg is a college student with Asperger Syndrome and a friend of Sasha's family. Sasha's parents want their daughter to learn advocacy skills, and they want her to learn from someone who is not them – they want to avoid learned dependence. Sasha has known Meg since she was a baby, and they like each other a great deal. Every Friday they get together, and, among other things, Sasha talks about what is good and bad about school. One day when Sasha tells Meg about the lights in the classroom making her eyes hurt, Meg helps Sasha make a list of possible solutions.

Sasha's first solution is to make them tear out the whiteboards and use lights like at home. In response to this rather extreme suggestion, Meg suggests that Sasha sit in a darker corner or wear a hat, to which Sasha says that she could wear sunglasses.

After making the list, Meg and Sasha decide what it is reasonable to ask for. No matter what Sasha and Meg say, the school is NOT going to redecorate for one little girl, so they cross off the idea about tearing out the whiteboards. Together, they decide to ask Sasha's teacher to move Sasha to a dimmer corner and to allow her to wear sunglasses in class.

Meg also goes over the concept of compromise with Sasha so she will be prepared in case the teacher does not accept their entire proposal. Meg makes sure Sasha knows that when making requests in situations like this, one usually has to compromise, giving up some of what one asks for. She explains that they are presenting several accommodations so that when the teacher wants to eliminate some of them and bargain, Sasha will still get her needs met.

Together, Meg and Sasha now decide *how* to ask. They discuss different ways they have asked people for things in the past, ranging from having tantrums to yelling to demanding to saying "please," and talk about the results of each one. Sasha says that all yelling ever does is get her sent to time-out, and Meg suggests that for something this big, a simple "please" is not sufficient. She guides Sasha to the idea of calmly explaining to the teacher what is bothering her and why, and politely asking for changes in her classroom accommodations. Meg asks Sasha questions to clarify what she experiences in the classroom. She also tells Sasha exactly what she is planning to say and makes sure she approves. They decide that Meg will pick Sasha up from school on Monday and will talk to the teacher at that time.

On Monday, Sasha and Meg approach the teacher. Meg makes sure to demonstrate conventional social skills in introducing herself, complimenting the teacher's work because she really is a good teacher, not just because it makes her more socially receptive. Besides, Meg would never lie in front of Sasha. She then calmly explains Sasha's visual difficulties and presents their proposed solutions to the problem. When the teacher questions her, Meg does not get defensive but answers in a rational, placid way. At the end, the teacher agrees to allow sunglasses and says she will move Sasha to a slightly dimmer spot, but she cannot lower the light level for her out of consideration for the other students. Meg quietly tells Sasha that this sounds like a fair compromise, and then asks her if she can agree to it. Sasha nods her head in agreement. Finally, Meg and Sasha both thank the teacher for her time and understanding and go back to Sasha's house.

In the car, Meg talks again about compromise and the importance of being calm in situations like this. She had been a good model but wants to make sure Sasha really gets those points. They talk about what went well and what could have been better, and then they plan their upcoming Friday get-together. Sasha loves ice cream, so they decide that next Friday they will go to the local ice cream parlor and talk about Sasha's week.

On the following Friday, Meg asks Sasha if her new accommodations are in place and if they are working. The answer is "yes" to both. If that had not been the case, they would have started the whole process over.

The above scenario clearly illustrates the modeling stage. The instructor (Meg) shows the budding advocate (Sasha) how to make requests, not because the neurotypical way is always better but because it increases the likelihood of needs being met. The reason for this is that there are more neurotypicals, not that their methods of getting things done and asking for favors or changes are necessarily the most efficient. The cliché "when in Rome, do as the Romans do" is appropriate to explain this concept. Although at times it seems as if Meg did things for Sasha, in actuality, Sasha was an active participant and observer. Also, her young age should be considered.

Stage 2: Facilitation and Confidence Building

In the second stage the new advocate is more active, but the facilitator is still very heavily involved. Stage 2 helps the student get used to presenting his or her needs orally or with the Picture Exchange Communication System (PECS) or some other alternative communication without the pressure of having to get it "exactly right." Rehearsal is an important component of this stage because advocacy is deceptively complex. Stage 2 can be as short as a day or as long as a decade, depending on the advocate's temperament and other personal differences.

Scenario

Cassidy used to love her dance class at a local studio. Now, sometimes when there is a lull in the action, Roberta and Lisa tease Cassidy for "standing funny" and "looking stupid." These two girls, like most kids, are very good at hiding the nasty things they do from adults so nobody is aware of what is going on. Roberta and Lisa pick on Cassidy in every class for two months, but one day Cassidy has had enough. She pushes Roberta into the mirror and kicks Lisa in the shin. Cassidy is expelled from dance class!

Self-Advocacy

Daniel takes a tumbling class from Cassidy's dance teacher. Roberta and Lisa are also in his class, and again tease and bully. Knowing that Daniel is tactile defensive, Roberta and Lisa like to gently touch him to make him squirm. They also tease him for being in a "girl sport" and for being one of the less coordinated kids in the class. This behavior makes Daniel very angry, so he tells his dad.

Daniel's dad wants to teach his son self-advocacy, so they make a plan. First they decide exactly what the problem is: Roberta and Lisa are not leaving Daniel alone. Then they brainstorm solutions. Their list includes: slugging Roberta and Lisa, telling their parents, quitting tumbling, asking the teacher to rearrange the line, changing class times, and "ignore it and it will go away."

After looking at their list, Daniel says that he does not think ignoring the girls would work. His dad thinks hitting Roberta and Lisa is a bad idea, so they remove that idea from the list too. Daniel really likes learning flips, so he does not want to quit, but he is willing to change class times if necessary. They both know that Roberta and Lisa's parents think their daughters are little angels, so the option of going to them is also quickly ruled out. Instead, Daniel and his dad decide first to talk to the teacher about rearranging the line to separate Daniel from the two girls.

Before they go, Daniel and his dad practice. They talk about compromise and calm communication. Quality time spent in honing the skills of compromise and communication will pay invaluable dividends for the novice self-advocate and as an adult, as explained in Roger Meyer's chapter, "Being Your Own Case Manager." Daniel and his dad write a script of what they will say, and they practice it over and over. Daniel's dad will get the teacher's attention and bring up the issues, then Daniel will fill in the details. They also role-play, with Daniel's dad asking Daniel the questions he thinks the tumbling teacher might ask, and they practice calm reactions in case the instructor cannot make any changes.

The next class, Daniel's dad takes his son to tumbling early so they can talk to the instructor. He approaches her, introduces himself and mentions that Daniel has been having problems with Roberta and Lisa. Then he asks Daniel to explain what goes on at practice. Daniel starts calmly, but soon begins to get agitated, so his dad squeezes his shoulders and takes over. The teacher likes Daniel because he is a hard worker and is very receptive to what he is told. As a result, she offers to talk to Roberta and Lisa and agrees to rearrange the line. She feels that since Roberta and Lisa are the problem, Daniel should not be the one to switch classes. They decide together that the teacher will discuss moving students to different classes if need be. After Daniel agrees that this is fair, he and his dad thank the teacher sincerely, and Daniel goes to class while his father watches.

During warm-ups, the instructor emphasizes to the whole class the rule of keeping hands to self, that tumbling is a class just like school and that, therefore, the students must behave and respect each other's differences. Roberta and Lisa try to stand next to Daniel, but the teacher arranges the line so that they are not near him or each other. When Lisa gets out of line and pokes Daniel in the back, she is made to run a lap because she is not behaving in a respectful manner – based on the conversation with Daniel and his dad, the instructor makes sure to watch the line more closely since she knows there is a problem. Often people genuinely want to help but do not know how, or even that it is necessary.

After class, Daniel and his father talk about the great response they got. Dad makes sure Daniel knows that responses to requests like this will not always be this stellar, but they might be sometimes. Every week after tumbling class Dad asks how it went, and the instructor tries to check in with Daniel every few weeks.

This stage is designed to build confidence. It is at this time that new advocates start practicing calm communication. The partner is still there to help in case the autistic advocate gets upset but does not play as intense a role as in Stage 1. The facilitator and the advocate are becoming more equal team members in carrying out the presentation, but the preparation is still heavily guided.

Stage 3: Partnering and Letter Writing

In this stage, the balance flips towards the autistic individual. If all goes well, the student now does most of the talking and is an equal partner in planning. Role-playing for rehearsal is started at this time. This stage is also a good time to introduce the very important tool of advocacy through letter writing.

Scenario

Jacob, age 13, feels that his parents treat him like a baby because he has autism. They do not know that this bothers him, but Jacob interprets their behavior to mean that they just do not care. Jacob begins to behave belligerently at home and, as a result, his parents take away his computer games for a week. Jacob storms up the stairs screaming about "baby punishments" and how his parents will not let him act his age.

Self-Advocacy

Jenna, Sam, Mike, and Christy are in Miss Thompson's social skills group for autistic and Asperger middle school students. They work on advocacy skills as a group. Like Jacob, both Sam and Christy think their parents are not letting them be teenagers. They have had some self-advocacy training before and it has helped, so they ask Miss Thompson to help them communicate better with their parents. Miss Thompson agrees, and asks Jenna and Mike if they will help Sam and Christy get ready.

First Miss Thompson asks Sam and Christy what they want their parents to change. Sam says he does not want his mother to follow him around "bugging him about everything," which includes reminding him to eat, sleep, do homework, bathe, and tie his shoes. Sam does have a significant problem remembering to do things, but he can use a visual schedule well at school and states he would prefer to use one at home too.

Christy is interested in going to school dances but does not think her parents will let her. She is very socially naive but well liked, so there is no social reason why it is unsafe for her to go. All the dances are well chaperoned, and her parents will pick her up immediately after each dance. A phone will also be available for Christy to contact them if she becomes overwhelmed. Besides, her sensory differences are such that severe overload at a junior high dance is unlikely.

Miss Thompson tells Sam and Christy that they have two options: they can talk to their parents or they can write a letter. She will help in either case. She explains that the advantages of writing a letter are that it is easier to stay calm while writing and making sure one says exactly what one means; however, it is easier for people to ignore and fail to read a letter. A face-to-face meeting, on the other hand, gets all questions cleared up and is harder to ignore, but it is easier to get upset and flustered when meeting in person.

Sam decides he wants to talk to his parents so he can answer all their concerns immediately. Christy chooses to write a letter because she wants to appear mature. She tends to get frustrated when questioned. The importance of letter writing is further discussed in Liane Willey's chapter, "Disclosure and Self-Advocacy: An Open Door Policy." As another option, Liane suggests using an agent to aid in disclosure and advocacy when meeting face-to-face is not practical.

Now that Sam and Christy have decided what option to choose, Miss Thompson has Sam, Jenna, and Mike role-play Sam's meeting. First they talk about communication. They practice doing it right, and then they try less effective ways. The kids have fun demonstrating the wrong way to talk to Sam's parents – yelling, stomping, being sarcastic, and pouting. After role-playing, Miss Thompson and Sam together write a short note to his parents requesting a brief meeting. They also create and practice a "help me" signal that Sam can use if he becomes flustered and wants Miss Thompson to take over.

While the other students are role-playing, Miss Thompson helps Christy write her letter. First Christy writes down everything she wants to say, then Miss Thompson helps her organize the list. After that, Christy writes all her points in grammatically correct, coherent sentences on the computer so editing is easier. When she thinks her letter is okay, Miss Thompson looks it over and they read it out loud. Christy hears one point that is not clear and two things that might sound "snotty," so she changes them, and they read the letter again. This time the letter expresses exactly what she meant to say. Christy prints out the letter and signs it, and puts it in a safe place to take it home.

The next time the group meets, Sam's parents come for the discussion with their son. Miss Thompson starts by saying that Sam has something to talk to them about. She then allows Sam to say what he has practiced. He gets frustrated at one question and signals to Miss Thompson as agreed, and she rescues him. Miss Thompson also clarifies certain points when Sam's parents look confused. She helps Sam use his visual aid, a picture schedule he had made. At first Sam's parents are skeptical, but they agree to try Sam's idea of using the visual schedule and, therefore, allow him to act more independently.

Christy gives her parents the letter as soon as she gets home. The next day, her parents ask to talk to her. She is very nervous because she did not practice answering questions. Luckily, they just want to say they had not known she was interested in dances, and they want to set ground rules but otherwise allow her to go. Christy would not have broken any of the guidelines her family set anyway, so she is very pleased with the response to her letter.

The next time they meet, Miss Thompson gets her group together to talk about Sam and Christy's successes. They talk about calm communication and about how it is very important to thank their parents. Sam also talks about how his mother started posting his chores on his schedule rather than telling him what to do when he was in the middle of doing in something else.

Even people who teach self-advocacy often expect new advocates to be able to go from a Stage 3 equivalent directly to fully independent expression of needs. However, the gap between the steps is way too big for most of us on the spectrum to bridge smoothly all at once. The last three stages build gradually to independent advocacy. These steps also lend themselves well to partnerships between budding advocates.

Stage 4: Moral Support

This stage focuses on "moral support." The person advocating will probably do all the talking, but the partner is there in case of emergency and to build confidence. The two partners still prepare together, but the person who is advocating no longer needs as much guidance as in the earlier stages. The moral support tends to range in physical proximity from nearly a shadow outside the door to waiting outside in a car, depending on the confidence of the advocate.

Scenario

Seventeen-year-old Will works at a grocery store after school. He used to do inventory and fill shelves, which he really liked. But recently, Will was moved to work at a cash register, which he detests "with a raging passion." The social interaction and sensory input are too much for him and, as a result, he is always overloaded after work.

One afternoon when Will's cash register jams, he becomes so upset that he runs out of the store. Afterwards, he is too embarrassed to return to work. Will knows a little about advocacy but does not know how to make it work for himself. He is good at troubleshooting other people's problems, but when he is emotionally and personally involved with a situation, he gets overwhelmed and needs guidance to solve the problem.

Self-Advocacy

Allison has been in Will's class for many years. They even shared an aide in elementary school, and they are good friends. Allison tutors on weekends to make money. She used to work with one child at a time, but her supervisor has recently put her in charge of three groups of five students each. One-on-one tutoring sessions meet in small quiet rooms, but in her new job assignment there are often three or four groups in the same large room at the same time. In that environment, Allison finds it difficult to concentrate and understand her students' questions. She asks Will to help her talk to her supervisor.

First Allison and Will prepare. Allison knows how to write letters, but she would prefer immediate feedback so she decides on a face-to-face meeting. She wants to ask to be moved back into the small rooms, but is willing to work with one or several kids at a time. Will agrees that this is reasonable, so they set up a meeting with Allison's boss.

Next, Allison and Will decide how Allison will broach the subject with her supervisor, and they talk about all the possible reactions she might get. They also role-play various scenarios so that Allison can practice staying calm.

When the meeting day arrives, Will goes with Allison. Since Allison finds deep pressure soothing, Will gives her a tight hug before they enter the room. Allison is also wearing a velvet shirt inside out under her sweater for soothing tactile stimulation. (Some autistic people choose to wear their velvet inside out because the outside is softer than the inside.) Will follows Allison into the meeting room.

At first, Allison is really nervous, so Will stays close as she begins. Since he can tell that she starts to relax as the discussion goes on, he soon wanders about the room looking at the wall decorations while Allison expresses her concerns. If he senses that Allison needs support, he comes back, but he wants to let her do what she can independently. After Allison and her boss finish, Allison thanks her for her time and heads out the door with Will.

Will and Allison discuss the results of the meeting. Her supervisor had no idea that the main room was so challenging for Allison and is putting her back tutoring one-to-one and two-to-one. She added that Allison is too valuable an employee to risk losing just because the environment does not work for her. Will and Allison decide that the meeting was a success because Allison stayed calm and did not make unreasonable or irrational requests or demands – and got the response she had hoped for.

Stage 4 can last a long time, because it is extremely variable. As mentioned, the person providing moral support can be right next to the advocate or outside the door, depending on the confidence of the advocate. For a letter writer, the moral support function involves reading the letter for tone and content at the request of the writer.

Stage 5: Taking the Lead

Stage 5 can last even longer than Stage 4. Besides, since it is very nearly independent, advocates who have advanced to Stage 6 sometimes return to Stage 5 for more difficult situations. In Stage 5, the autistic advocate leads the way. While another party helps with the preparation, he or she only follows the advocate's wishes. That is, the autistic writes the letter or holds the meeting alone, using the preparation he or she practiced with a partner.

Scenario

Randy takes a music appreciation class at a local community college. The instructor often gives oral quizzes, which Randy does poorly on because of auditory processing problems. The sound system in the classroom is extremely intense, and it hurts Randy's ears – sometimes the pain gets so bad that he wants to throw up during music class. Randy's older brother, Matt, is also autistic and tried once to take the same class. He dropped the course because similar problems led him to skip classes, heading him towards failure due to lack of attendance. Randy does not want to leave the class, so he asks Matt to help him come up with a workable solution.

Self-Advocacy

Randy wants to talk to the music teacher alone, but he needs help in preparing to do so. He asks Matt if it is reasonable to request written quizzes and permission to wear earplugs to class. Since Randy gets accommodations through the college disability services, he knows these are very reasonable requests. Both men realize that the music teacher does not often read written correspondence, so Randy decides to talk to him in person. In preparation, Matt role-plays the way they think the teacher might act so that Randy can practice answering objections. Randy plans to talk to his teacher after the next class.

The professor knows that Randy takes his tests in another room, but he does not know the nature of his disability. When Randy approaches him and tells him that the sound system is painful and that he has difficulty with oral quizzes as a result, the professor does not understand. Then Randy explains autism in the way he had practiced with Matt. Once the instructor has gained a better understanding, he is open to making slight modifications, including giving him quizzes on paper rather orally. Randy makes sure to thank his music teacher for his time then and subsequently every time he makes a change for Randy's benefit.

In another example of taking the lead, Matt wrote a letter about his autism to request a more consistent schedule at his job. Without a consistent schedule, Matt gets very stressed out and does not perform as well. He tends to forget his duties and make mistakes. But his error rate is very low if he does the same thing every day. He has revised this letter three times, but he wants to make sure it does not sound rude to other people. Randy reads the letter over for his brother, and when he has no suggestions, Matt sends it and is very pleased at the resulting changes at work.

Stage 6: Independent Self-Advocacy

Although many of us prefer to receive help preparing for advocacy, sometimes we have to do the whole process on our own. Once we reach adulthood, we do not always have someone around who is knowledgeable about autism and the kind of advocacy help we need. Adult autistics may have to advocate for themselves at work, in college, with government agencies, even among autism groups, and many other places. Independent self-advocacy is the final stage of learning to get one's needs met. In this stage, the advocate undertakes all preparation, presentation, and evaluation.

Scenario

Beth is an autistic adult who sometimes attends meetings of the local parent autism organization. While the leaders genuinely like having Beth attend, others in the group do not, because she challenges their idea of autism and because she speaks out against cures and certain treatments. They are either rude or patronizing towards her. In an autism organization, least of all, Beth should not have to put up with bad attitudes, so she makes a plan to advocate for herself.

Self-Advocacy

First Beth calls the leaders of the group. She tells them she has been having problems and that she wants to talk to the offenders. She takes the precaution of calling ahead of time in case someone later complains that she was mean. Then she writes down everything she wants to say. After that she has to decide how to present her case.

Sometimes Beth writes articles for the organization's newsletter, so she considers writing an article. However, since not everyone reads the newsletter, and not everyone is causing a problem, Beth decides this is not the best option for making her point. She feels she will get better results if she directly confronts those who have been rude to her.

After Beth looks over her points again, she realizes that she has great fodder for an article about how people expect their autistic children to be treated well, but at the same time neglect to respect the right of adult autistics to be treated civilly. Because the thought will not leave her head, Beth decides to write the article and submit it, but also decides to speak individually to the mothers who have been impolite to her.

Beth practices with the mirror every day for a week. She practices what she will say to the women 50 times, and then screams what she *really* wants to say once to get it out of her system. After that she practices the polite way 15 more times. The day of the next autism meeting, Beth does her favorite sensory activities to calm herself and puts her favorite rock in her pocket to fidget with.

After the meeting, Beth approaches the problem mother who is the least obnoxious and states her case. The mother claims not to have realized that she treated Beth in a patronizing manner, and promises she will try to relate to her as an adult. She is new to autism, and is used to talking to her autistic son the way she had been talking to Beth. Beth has just turned the first mother into an ally with the potential of transforming the others as well. Phil Schwarz, in his chapter, "Building Alliances: Community Identity and the Role of Allies in Autistic Self-Advocacy," offers techniques for forming alliances with others and shows the benefits to both the individual and autistic community.

Encouraged by this success, Beth decides to talk to the meanest parent while her confidence is high. This does not go as well because this mom has a problem with all "successful" autistics, not just Beth, because they challenge her idea of autism; besides, her child is considered lower functioning. Upon learning that, Beth knows that the problem is no longer hers and decides to alert the leaders of the organization if the need arises. She then talks to the other two rude parents with a modicum of success, and finally hopes that her article will have a stronger impact.

Once the newsletter with her article comes out, Beth has another opportunity to evaluate the response to her advocacy efforts. This is not difficult, because everyone has a strong reaction to her writing: some people, including the first mother, express a newfound respect for Beth, others demonstrate various intensities of anger with her – some of the parents are irritated, one mother yells at Beth. Reasons for their irritation span from feeling that newsletter space could have been better used for other articles to being offended at Beth's writing. The leaders do not object to what Beth wrote, or they would not have published her words, so Beth decides that her best course of action now is to stay away from the people who clearly do not like her.

Although all the preceding examples included people who use speech fairly well, nonverbal autistics can also learn advocacy. PECS, typing, sign language and other alternative modes of communication can all be used in advocacy much the same way speech can. All six steps of the advocacy learning process can be adapted to an individual's abilities and methods of communication. No one should be denied the chance to speak and advocate for him or herself because of communication differences, and no one should be denied the chance to learn advocacy because of autism. The above detailed process can be started at any age and can be used at any rate. Advocacy is one of the most important independence skills we autistics can learn.

Situational Self-Advocacy

Not all advocacy covers the kind of situations where one ideally only has to make one's needs met once. Often we find ourselves making the same need known repeatedly to many different people. Examples include checking ingredients at a restaurant because of food allergies and sensitivities, getting a special assistance pass because lines are too overstimulating at an amusement park, going through airport security because we tend to look suspicious and get pulled out of line – a sensory nightmare – or attending a movie. There is an infinite range of situations where one may have to advocate for oneself, and the kinds of situations you will come across depend on your interests and activities.

My preferred method for situational advocacy is to write a letter. To prepare and save time, I have a collection of letters that I use for differ-

---

Sample Letter: Restaurants

To Whom It May Concern:

I am a new patron at your establishment, and I have severe food sensitivities. For me to find something safe to eat, I or someone else must read the ingredients of everything that goes into what I order. Even trace amounts of some of the offending substances will cause problems. I would very much appreciate efforts to avoid them in my meal.

Ingredients I am allergic to include:
- All food dyes, especially Red 40 and Yellow 5
- Artificial flavoring, including vanillin (but vanilla is safe)
- BHA, BHT, and TBHQ
- Curly endive, red apples, red or purple grapes, pineapple
- Aspartame
- Shrimp

Although this list appears daunting, most people are surprised at how much I can actually eat. Thank you for you cooperation.

Sincerely,

Kassiane A. Sibley

---

ent situations. The advantages of letters are that the advocate is less likely to leave something out, and they also eliminate the need for verbal communication in potentially stressful situations. At times verbal explanations and requests are more efficient, but which method an individual chooses is based solely on preference and effectiveness; no one method is right for everyone.

Dietary Restrictions

A large number of people with autism spectrum disorders have dietary restrictions because of allergies or sensitivities, resulting in the need to check the ingredients of anything they ingest. One girl I know has such restrictions, and once when she did not get a favorable answer to her request that a restaurant cater to her dietary needs, she had a major meltdown. I also have food sensitivities, but I know that if I had a meltdown of that magnitude, I would likely be arrested, so I have developed more effective strategies.

The first strategy I used was to ask to see ingredients lists. The answer was usually that no such list was available, but the wait staff were often willing to check for me. Then I listed my myriad sensitivities, and they asked the kitchen staff about specific items for me. I have had several adverse reactions to this approach, so I moved to a new strategy.

My second tactic was to carry a small, reinforced index card listing all the offending ingredients. I could hand this to the staff and ask them to check the food or beverage for what was written on the card. This worked well until the index card disintegrated in the wash. At that point, I wrote a letter with similar information and have been carrying that around instead.

In my experience, most people react favorably to written expression of food sensitivities. I have had someone refuse to check ingredients for me exactly once, at which time I demonstrated very poor advocacy skills and had a meltdown. The meltdown was brought on in part by frustration, in part by low blood sugar. But usually I get a very helpful response to my card or letter. Writing down allergies and sensitivities makes them seem more legitimate, making it easier to obtain the information that enables you to select something safe to eat.

Special Assistance Passes

More and more people on the autistic spectrum go to amusement parks. For those of us who crave movement, a roller coaster can be sensory heaven, but the line to get on a ride can be sensory hell. Most parks now offer a special assistance pass, but often employees hesitate to give it to people with invisible disabilities. It seems that the philosophy is that if someone can ask for a pass, he or she is not disabled "enough" to get one.

This is where the letter comes in. A written document explaining autism and sensory issues along with documentation of diagnosis can go a long way in securing a pass. Such a pass can mean the difference between a successful trip and the most awful day of several people's lives – your own, your friends and your family.

Sample Letter: Amusement Park

To Whom It May Concern:

My name is Kassiane Alexandra Sibley and I have a form of autism. Autism is a neurological condition first noticed in childhood that causes difficulty with socialization, communication, and sensory processing. Although autism is first noticed in childhood, it is a life-long condition. Therefore, adults can also be autistic.

Autism is a hidden disability, which means I look like everyone else although I do not process like everyone else. Because of my condition, I cannot deal with large crowds of people, loud noises, sudden touch, or chaotic environments such as those present in an amusement park line. Although I am neither aggressive nor dangerous, if I am startled or overwhelmed, I may reflexively lash out. This is not violence; it is an intense startle reflex. Amusement park attractions themselves have a calming effect. However, the lines are precisely the kind of environment that leads to severe overload and heightening of my startle.

Enclosed is a letter of my diagnosis of Asperger Syndrome, my form of autism, from Dr. John Ratey of Harvard Medical School.

In addition to autism, I have severe food sensitivities. It is not always possible to purchase food that fits my special needs. Because of this difficulty and the severity of my sensitivities, I find it best to bring my own food and leave it in the first aid center until meal times.

Thank you very much for your consideration in dealing with my special needs. If you have any questions, please ask and they will be answered.

Sincerely,

Kassiane A. Sibley
Peoria, Illinois

Airport Security

Airport security has become an ordeal for everyone, whether they have neurosocial differences or not. Unfortunately, due to our autistic characteristics, we are much more likely to be searched because we are perceived as acting suspicious (Debbaudt, 2001). Sensory and crowd issues make us behave even more strangely than we usually do, so we have a target on our foreheads in the eyes of security screeners. In other words, we give off nonverbal messages that are contrary to what the Transportation Security Administration considers consistent with a safe person.

In her chapter, "Communicating Through Advocacy and Self-Disclosure: Four Ways to Connect," Ruth Elaine Hane discusses her intrusive experiences with airport security. By observing how her behaviors contrast with other people's nonverbal cues in an airport, Ruth Elaine learned how to get through security with minimal hassle. Ruth Elaine offers valuable information on getting to know oneself better – a prerequisite for advocating for one's needs.

According to the FAA website, http://www.tsa.gov/public/interapp/editorial/editorial_1374.xml>, persons with disabilities have the right to inform checkpoint personnel of their disability, which provides persons on the autism spectrum an opportunity to educate others of our differences and needs. For example, (a) we have a brain-based difference that makes eye contact alien to us; (b) we need to have procedures explained before they occur; and (c) we do better if we are not touched. However, reciting all of this in a world where "autism" still is seen to mean "nonverbal and rocking in a corner" is likely to get us searched even more.

Instead, I use a letter that Sarah Knudsen, an autistic friend of mine wrote (see p. 53) that simply explains the pertinent effects autism has on my potential interactions with security personnel. I used the same document when a police officer pulled me over for speeding one time. While I do not know if the letter made the officer more lenient, at least it did not seem to aggravate him. The letter included highlights of my particular areas of difficulty. Others may find that they need to include other points as well. The information on this letter can also be placed on an index card or a business card.

I also have a letter (see p. 54) for people who need more information, such as emergency personnel or those who might call emergency personnel if they do not understand what is going on. This letter includes contact information for people to call if I am so overstimulated that I cannot safely remove myself from the situation, as well as pertinent medical information. If the brief letter will not get me through a situation, or if I feel that I need

---

Sample Index Card: General Information

I am autistic. This means I do not make eye contact well or sound like most people. This also means I have difficulty with the following:

- eye contact
- bright or flashing lights
- sudden sounds
- light or unexpected touches.

I am not aggressive or dangerous, but I may not react as you expect in certain situations. Please inform me of what you plan to do before you do it. If you are going to touch me, please say, "I need to touch your shoulder," for example, and then use a firm touch. Thank you.

---

help, this is the letter to use. If I am too overloaded to decide which letter is appropriate, that means I probably need to use this one. Because it has medical information, I keep it where someone looking for identification would find it.

Medical Community

Sometimes it is necessary for autistic people to advocate for themselves to medical professionals. Many of us are highly sensitive to medication, making experimenting with different psychoactive agents very unpredictable. Doctors must understand that a very small amount of a substance can have a more intense effect on the autistic system than a larger amount in a neurotypical person. Although advocating with a doctor regarding pills and procedures can be extremely awkward because the physician is supposed to be the expert, many highly unpleasant situations can be avoided this way.

For example, I know that I am extremely sensitive to anything that has the slightest stimulant effect. Since I am also unbelievably hyperactive, many doctors think I would benefit from a medication for ADHD. But the vast majority of those compounds are stimulants, which I cannot take. I have had to learn to tell professionals this instead of letting them prescribe yet another pill that would make me miserable. For some people, the consequences of not telling doctors about their sensitivities to substances can be even greater than they are in my case.

Sample Letter: Emergency Situations

To the Person to Whom I Hand This Letter:

If you are reading this letter, I am probably already acting in an unusual manner. My name is Kassiane Sibley, and I have a neurological condition known as autism. Because of my condition, I behave differently from most people, although I look normal.

When I am mildly stressed, I might rock or make movements with my hands. I also do not look at people. If I am severely stressed, I may become nonverbal or talk way too much. Sometimes I completely forget how to talk.

Sensory stimuli can feel very intense to me. If you must talk to me, please do so in a quiet voice. Even if I have headphones on, I can hear you. Please do not touch me without warning me first, and then do so only if absolutely necessary. If you have to touch me, please do so firmly. I do not tolerate flashing lights well either, and might appear to panic.

Usually I will calm down on my own. I am neither dangerous nor disturbed, but just have a different way of dealing with stress. If you feel that this is an emergency situation, please call (emergency contact) at (XXX)XXX-XXXX. If they are not available or I am traveling, please refer to the attached sheet for the nearest emergency contact. If I need to go to a hospital, an Order of Saint Francis hospital is my first choice. Also, I take Topamax, Neurontin, Risperdal, and Strattera and am allergic to stimulants, food dye, and Lamictal. If I will be safe calming down at a nearby, quiet location, that is preferable to calling anyone.

Thank you for your understanding,

Kassiane A. Sibley

Movie Theaters

Movies are a great pastime year-round in the Midwest where I live due to the freezing cold in the winter or summer heat that would fry an egg. Once I started making friends and going to movies, I found that theaters tended to be extremely loud. Also, the green lighting my local theater uses to illuminate the stadium-seating makes me dizzy and disoriented, if not downright nauseated.

At the movie theater, I favor verbal advocacy because it would take a several-page letter to cover all situations. I do have a letter for sound levels, but have only used it once. Usually when going to a theater, I have someone with me to help me not fall on the stairs. I then talk to a manager if the sound is too loud or a light is flickering, which is another sensitivity of mine. For example, just saying "the sound in Theater 4 is really loud, would it be possible to turn it down some?" usually results in the theater manager correcting the situation.

Occasionally when the lights are flashing, I have had to make mention of seizure disorders among movie patrons, but sound is usually the main problem. If a person on the spectrum is so sound sensitive that her ideal listening level is much lower than a comfort level for other moviegoers, I recommend against the advocacy route and instead suggest making one's own accommodations. For example, I carry sound-canceling headphones with me for situations such as this.

Being reasonable is a key for successful self-advocacy. It is reasonable to want to know what is in my dinner or not be touched in the line at the airport. It is NOT reasonable for me to make them turn the movie volume down so low that it causes everyone else to need headsets. Our rights and needs cannot trample on the rights of others.

Nonverbal Advocacy

Sometimes autistic persons, even fairly skilled advocates, can get so stressed that they are unable to express their needs effectively. What makes a person anxious or flappy to the point of losing verbal ability tends to be consistent within that person. For example, if I am driving and get pulled over, I WILL forget how to talk. That is a very high-stress situation for me, and no matter what, I will go nonverbal. Different people have different forget-how-to-talk situations, but they will probably stay the same. Augmentative communication strategies are a good way of getting needs met when one becomes nonverbal due to stress.

Many people on the autistic spectrum learn to talk using cards with pictures on them. Even if they begin speaking fluently, it may be a good idea to maintain the communication book and keep it handy. While a communication book might be unwieldy, dragging it around is much better than being stranded somewhere unable to make one's needs known. People who maintain one of these systems must make sure they have the appropriate icons. Generally, it does little good to have myriad pictures of food and toys once the user can ask for these items verbally. More useful icons would include the emergency contact's picture, name and phone number, a symbol for "Don't touch me," and other things one needs to communicate when stressed to the point of becoming nonverbal.

An offshoot of pictures are cards with important pieces of information, such as name, food issues, "I'm Autistic," and queries or directions like "Don't touch me." I wish this was my idea, but it is not. Eileen Torchio, an autistic friend, came up with the idea of cards at an autism conference, and they usually produce spectacular results. For a while I carried around a packet of these cards on a key chain hung on my belt loop. They were very useful while they lasted, but my poor effort at laminating eventually caused all the cards to fall off the metal loop. So I recommend "professional" laminating.

Some autistic people wear medical-alert-type jewelry with a message indicating they are on the spectrum. Others choose to carry a business card-sized message stating that they have autism, that they are not dangerous, but that they do not think, feel, or perceive the way typical people do. When people make these tools themselves, they can include the specific issues they have the most trouble with on the reverse side of the card. Most of the commercially made cards are for parents of autistic children to hand out when their children embarrass them, but it is possible to modify the idea for an adult who needs to explain his or her behavior.

My latest strategy for nonverbal advocacy includes creating even more letters. I carry a general one about autism, in addition to the ones mentioned earlier. A letter can be more detailed than a card or bracelet, but it is also more likely to dissolve in the wash. In this day of computers and ease of saving one's work, this is not as problematic as it would have been in the age of the typewriter. A letter can be well organized and tailored to the autistic individual's needs. Some persons do not like to read a letter handed to them, but most people genuinely want to help, so the letter works.

One more useful nonverbal tool is sign language. I have learned about 12 "survival signs," including "I'm autistic," "I'm overwhelmed," and "I can hear but not talk." The biggest drawback is that few people understand sign language. Also, when I use sign language, most people assume I am deaf and try to find an interpreter and/or something to write on in an effort to communicate. However, even if this does not have the intended results, if this means they are writing instead of yelling at me, that is no bad thing when I am overloaded anyway. This method is completely useless for some people because if they get too upset for speech, all language goes. However, there are some occasions when sign language can be a life saver for an autistic advocate. Again, the effectiveness of this mode of communication as a tool for self-advocacy depends on the person and the particular circumstances.

Spreading Awareness as a Tool for Self-Advocacy

Practice and nonverbal tools can make advocacy easier. There is another way to help all autistics get their needs met: spreading awareness. The more the general public knows about what autism really is rather than the movie versions, the more likely they are to accommodate our differences. There are many ways to let the world know about autism.

Big Events

There are big ways people try to raise awareness. Usually the people involved with these events are neurologically typical parents of autistic children, and the awareness they are aiming for is not the kind that gets adults the help we need. Most of us cannot afford to hold big rallies about adult autism, nor do we have the resources for commercials, public service announcements, or television fundraisers involving celebrities. But we have a wealth of our own knowledge and personal experience. This does not sound like much, but the little things mentioned in this chapter as well as throughout the book can make a difference in our everyday lives.

Public Speaking

Yet another way I have spread awareness is by talking about my experiences to college classes and local autism support groups. Textbooks and parent group speakers often restrict their focus to the "catastrophe" autism represents and to children. My presentations allow me to highlight the positive aspects, while also pointing out the areas where I need environmental adjustments or other accommodations to be successful as an adult. The problem with talking to these kinds of groups is that their members tend to be at least moderately aware anyway and sometimes already have set ideas in their minds, making it harder to effect change than to educate someone who has never heard of autism.

Fliers and Fact Sheets

An offshoot of public speaking is handing out fliers or fact sheets about autism and the needs of autistic people. This involves some social interaction in addition to the cost of printing the fliers, but it can reach a large number of people who may not have a clue about the autism spectrum. Before distributing information in a public place, it is important to secure permission to avoid legal issues.

Wearable Propaganda

My favorite way to spread information about autism is using myself as a walking billboard: wearable propaganda! T-shirts or sweatshirts, buttons, and the like, all fall under this heading. Shirts can be obtained online through http://www.cafeshops.com under the searches "autism" and "Asperger." The Nth Degree (http://www.thenthdegree.com) also sells cool shirts about a variety of disabilities, but none specifies autism at this time.

Another option is to create your own shirt economically by ironing on a computer-printed design using iron-on paper or fabric paint. Using the paints can be a perilous proposition for those of us with fine-motor challenges. Using a computer-based program gives one infinite tries to make the design look right. Almost everyone wears and reads t-shirts, so this is a painless way to spread knowledge about whatever aspect of autism one thinks the public needs to know about.

Letter Writing

Writing letters to elected officials is a good way to gradually increase awareness of the autism spectrum. As for most of the general public, however, stories of autism that come to the attention of a majority of government officials are cries of "fix my kid" from disgruntled parents, giving the politicians a skewed picture of a tremendously suffering, perpetually dependent child who causes endless heartache to his family and friends. This bleak image of autism is not conducive to getting adult needs met, and encourages learned helplessness by promoting the image that individuals with autism cannot learn to do things for themselves.

Adult autistics need services and provisions appropriate to their age, which are often different than for a child. In addition to independent-living issues and the many human rights controversies surrounding autism, politicians have to be made aware that capable adult autistics exist and have opinions on those topics. Thus, speaking out about issues impacting us now is yet another way of advocating for ourselves as well as for future generations.

Advocacy Groups

Self-advocacy is an important skill for all people to learn, but most especially for those of us with autistic spectrum conditions and other hidden disabilities and differences for whom these skills usually do not come naturally, and whose communication skills are not always inherently effective. We have to learn to advocate for ourselves and also help those who will follow in our footsteps.

Starting an advocacy focus group is a way to work on the skills required for advocacy. It is easier to see solutions to another's problems as one is not personally invested. In other words, it is usually easier to advocate effectively for others than for oneself, at least in the beginning of advocacy skill development. In addition to getting our needs met, a group of adult autistics learning to stand up for their rights offers a social, community-building opportunity. Another advantage is that the various members of a group can provide numerous perspectives on difficulties an individual might be having, thereby helping to come up with a solution.

An autistic person, or a parent thereof, might want to start a group to teach children to advocate for their needs. Ideal advocacy teaching starts as soon as a family knows a child is on the spectrum. Adult autistics with fair to excellent advocacy skills can be great facilitators of such groups. Many times parent support groups do not think about teaching self-advocacy, yet in my experience, once they hear of the opportunity, they are enthusiastic. The challenge is that families of autistics say that they want us to lead independent lives, but usually with the prerequisite that we become typical people instead of teaching us to work with what we have.

The success of a self-advocacy group for children depends on the prevailing attitudes of the parents. Some parents see self-advocacy groups as an excellent social and learning opportunity whereas others see them as an undermining of the family, with most reactions falling somewhere in the middle. The same applies to adults still living with their families or under guardianship. Those who would most benefit from direct advocacy instruction are the ones least likely to gain access to it. The teenagers in the Stage 3 example earlier were part of one of these types of groups.

Partnerships

If large groups are not your cup of tea, you may benefit from partnering with another autistic person, like Allison and Will did in the Stage 4 example. A partnership can be formal or informal, temporary or long-standing, and can be based on friendship, having a situation in common, or simply being the only two adult autistic people in the area.

There are many reasons to enter a relationship in addition to working on advocacy, just as there are endless reasons to advocate in the first place. There are definite advantages to a partnership setup, particularly a long-standing one. The two partners are likely to grow quite close if they work together often, which benefits those who crave friendship. As the partners grow closer, they can learn about their own strengths and weaknesses as well as those of their advocacy buddy. Practicing the skills necessary to get one's needs met can be fun once good rapport has been established. Disadvantages stem mainly from mismatches of partners, or if one partner is domineering and persuades the other to use a course of action not best suited to his or her strengths and needs.

Effective ways to find a partner span from getting together with someone from school to posting an advertisement at a college's disability services office to attending a local autism organization's meeting and talking to any other autistics present. These are only suggestions, and there are many other ways to find an advocacy partner.

Mentoring

Some autistic people, especially those who have already learned to advocate fairly well, enjoy mentoring a younger person on the spectrum. Meg and Sasha in the Stage 1 story are an example of such an arrangement. Both parties can gain much that is positive from this kind of experience. Contrary to the belief of many professionals that we lack empathy, many of us relate well to children and teens with autistic spectrum conditions. Using our experience to help another can be gratifying, particularly if it can spare the younger generation some of the pain we have had to live through.

The younger partner gets rewards from the partnership, too. He or she learns to advocate and gets a mentor, who can be like an older sibling, a role model, or perhaps both. The child or teen learns from the mentor's extensive life experience on the spectrum within a neurologically typical world. When considering such an arrangement, be sure to get parental consent first. If a parent or guardian does not approve of the mentor or the idea of autistics learning from autistics, the relationship could get awkward. Another possible disadvantage could be personality conflict between the older and younger partners.

Adults with autism who are interested in working on advocacy skills with a child can go to a support meeting to see if they can pick up any pointers from parents who wish to teach their children to advocate for themselves. Another way would be to call parents who are looking for in-home therapists and explain that you are not interested in doing a behavioral program but that you have autism and would like to mentor. Some special education programs might be willing to give out contact information to parents who they feel might be interested.

Posting an advertisement at a community college student support office might be helpful or scouting out autism organization meetings, presuming the group in question is autistic-friendly and include parents wanting to find a potential autistic mentor for their child.

IEP

Another vehicle that helps children on the spectrum learn self-advocacy is the IEP, as discussed in Stephen's chapter, "The IEP as a Tool for Building Skills in Self-Advocacy." Ideally, teaching advocacy would be so ingrained in all curricula that there would be no need to mention it on the IEP, but that is not the way the system works at this time. Parents can see to it that self-advocacy skills are directly written into the IEP under the heading of daily living skills, for example. An expert in special education could help in getting a self-advocacy curriculum written and implemented.

Options for Those Who Want to Work Alone

Options for those who prefer to work alone are many. Internet discussions of advocacy are one such option. There are also many ways to advocate, directly or indirectly, that do not require any interaction at all. An individual who enjoys designing t-shirts or sweatshirts, for example, can sell her art on the Internet. Letter writing can be done in solitude, as can writing articles for local autism groups or newspapers. The options are endless.

The Importance of Attitude

No matter what someone chooses to do for advocacy, attitude is important! An individual who starts every advocacy project with a "me versus them," hostile confrontational mindset will more than likely run into obstacles and barriers. Although there are some people who do not want to learn or cannot understand, most of the world is made up of good but often misguided people who genuinely want to be helpful. Those who have neurological typicality do not instinctively know about autism, just as autistic people do not instinctively learn social patterns. Often people who are trying to help but end up making things worse do not realize they are doing so.

If we approach this with the attitude that the typical world is out to make our lives difficult, or with the mindset that people who do not know what we need are stupid, we will come across as hostile or condescending, thereby lowering the chances of successful advocacy. If, on the other hand, an advocate approaches the situation in an educational, matter-of-fact, calm manner, it is much easier to get favorable results. Typical people also prefer requests to demands. Even if something is technically a demand, wording it as a question makes it seem more optional to them. If helping is an option, most people will do so gladly – it is when they are forced to change something that they may start to regret it. This is based on much personal experience, but seems to hold true for the vast majority of people.

The gift of advocacy is the most important gift we can give to ourselves and the next generation. Some day there will not be anyone around to help get our needs met. We are experts about our own needs and are, therefore, the ones who should be explaining our issues and ways to work around them. A well-meaning neurotypical person may know autism as a whole, but will not know autism as it applies to the individual in question. Advocacy is an individualized process, and especially with autistic spectrum conditions, one set of accommodations does not fit all. Outside advocates too often focus on the negative, but those who advocate for themselves can point out the strengths and the weaknesses they possess as part of this beautiful, varied spectrum.

Kassiane Alexandra Sibley *is an independent young adult, tumbling coach, special education major, tutor to children on the autism spectrum, and co-teacher of a ballet class for autistic and Asperger children. She has spoken locally and nationally and has also published articles in several publications, and never misses a chance to spread public awareness. Like many Aspies her age, Kassiane was improperly diagnosed before discovering the autism spectrum at the age of 18. In addition to her autism activities, Kassiane competes in power tumbling, for which she recently won the Amanda Howe Sunshine Memorial Award for Sportsmanship.*

References

Debbaudt, D. (2001). *Autism, advocates, and law enforcement professionals: Recognizing and reducing risk situations for people with autism spectrum disorders.* London: Jessica Kingsley Publishers.

CHAPTER 3

Using the IEP to Build Skills in Self-Advocacy and Disclosure

Stephen M. Shore

Martin has just graduated high school and, boy, is he proud! His early days in school were difficult, and he spent a lot of time in a "special" room. By high school he was in general education classes thanks to the support of aides. Additionally, Martin received much academic support and encouragement from his parents. Graduating with a B average, he was very excited to attend a state university almost 100 miles from his home.

College started off well. Martin roomed with a high school friend in the dorm and was genuinely surprised that people whom he did not even know would talk with him – sometimes late into the night – about classes, interests, and life in general. Classes were interesting, taught by dedicated professors, and students were committed to learning. The difficulties of public school and the special treatment Martin had received soon became but a distant memory. Special education was "all done." Martin had achieved his goal of being just like everyone else. He was a regular guy.

At the beginning of the semester, Martin earned respectable grades on a few quizzes, but the coursework soon started getting harder. Midterm brought a couple of cumulative tests, a project, and a paper. Low grades as he had seen in high school started returning. His work no longer seemed to be at the level he started the semester with. Martin became anxious, and the mere thought of going to class to face the now confusing set of expectations was sometimes enough to send him into a panic attack. As a result, he became depressed and only attended classes irregularly.

Taking note of the wide range of Martin's abilities and challenges, one of his professors suggests that Martin go to the college disability office. With much reluctance, he makes an appointment. Depressed and very apprehensive, Martin meets with the disability counselor a week later. He wonders if it is going to be like public school special education all over again. He tells the counselor that although college started off very well, he now finds it difficult to work at the level expected of him. He admits that he is confused and frightened at what his dream of college has become.

When the counselor asks about a disability and whether he received special education at school, Martin indicates that he received special education services but he was not sure why. The counselor proceeds to list a number of conditions such as ADHD, dyslexia, and even Asperger Syndrome, but Martin still does not know if any of them apply to him.

The counselor schedules another session in a week's time and asks Martin to obtain the following information from his parents in the meantime:

1. *Diagnosis from public school*
2. *What services he received*
3. *Other relevant documentation*

Upon researching into his past, Martin finds out that he was originally diagnosed with autism, which was changed to Asperger Syndrome at about age 13. His most recent assessment took place at the end of middle school.

At Martin's second meeting with the counselor, he is informed that the college has the facilities to offer the needed accommodation, but that the disabilities office will not offer help until he can submit a more recent (within three years) neuropsychological assessment-based diagnostic report. Martin finds out that the soonest he can schedule such an exam is eight months away. Frustrated, he drops out of school.

W hat happened to Martin? In few words, he was not informed of his condition early in life and not given the opportunity to assist in planning his own education.

The above scenario happens all too often to people whose conditions are hidden from them. His parents and educators did not actively teach Martin how to best live *with* his condition. Instead, it was viewed with shame and, therefore, something to be hidden. Martin was not prepared to deal with the paradigm shift from being advocated for in the public schools to having to advocate for himself. Like Martin, many students fail to initiate a search for accommodations at the college level or other aspects of adult life because they never had the opportunity to do so in the public schools (Lynch & Gussel, 1996).

When I was in school, there was no individualized education program (IEP). In fact, especially in the lower grades, I was most likely viewed as this odd child whom other students picked on, who made strange sounds in the classroom, had difficulty learning class material, and engaged in a number of unusual interests. Most of my primary school days were spent in solitary pursuit of my own interests and being bullied by other children. Although I talked to some teachers and lunch monitors about the bullying, it never occurred to me to tell my parents what went on in school, nor that there was something that could be done about it. For many people on the autism spectrum, it does not occur to us that a bad situation can be made better, much less how to go about doing so.

As far as disclosure is concerned, I had it easy; at least in the beginning. My parents have used the word "autism" for as long as I can remember. Rather than being something to hide, autism was the reason why I went to a special school and saw certain doctors once a week, and it was also the basis of why public school was so difficult. By college, I considered autism as "all done," and its effects on me became a hazy, distant memory. It was not until the end of a doctoral program in music education that I had to face the awakening dragon of autism hissing in my face, telling me that autism and I still had the rest of my life to be together. The time had arrived to rebuild an identity that included autism to more accurately reflect my interactions and interpretations with the world; in short, a very different yet more fulfilling way of looking at life.

Self-advocacy and disclosure are inexorably linked because the need for self-advocacy begins when a person's needs are not being met in a given situation. Part of self-advocacy involves educating others of one's needs, and that usually includes reasons why; hence disclosure. The challenge is to accomplish this self-advocacy and disclosure in a way that promotes better mutual understanding (Shore, 2003a) and, therefore, benefits all involved. For example, after telling my wife *why* the ticking of an alarm clock was so troubling, she was able to have much greater empathy for my situation and remove the offending device.

Having a vehicle for developing skills in self-advocacy and appropriate disclosure while in public school will pay great dividends in self-awareness and interfacing with the world as a "different" person later on. After working through my own challenges of self-advocacy and disclosure, I now wish to use my experiences to help others on the autism spectrum develop badly needed skills in self-advocacy and disclosure. The IEP is a great way to start this work.

The goal of this chapter is to help persons on the autism spectrum, teachers, school administrators, parents, and others, explore the use of the IEP is an agent for developing self-advocacy and disclosure skills in children on the autism spectrum. For students to get effectively involved in their own IEP requires the collaboration and agreement of all of the people listed above. For this reason I have addressed the chapter to the significant people in the lives of those with autism.

All who are interested in using the IEP as a vehicle for developing skills in self-advocacy and disclosure may want to start by reading the question-and-answer introduction to the major aspects of the IEP on pages 69-70 from *A Student's Guide to the IEP* published by the National Information Center for Children and Youth with Disabilities (McGahee-Kovac, 2002).

Getting Started

Start Early

When is it appropriate to begin teaching the concepts of self-advocacy and disclosure? There is no hard and fast answer. In general, the best time to start teaching the concepts of self-advocacy and disclosure is when it is first learned that a child has a condition and deemed in need of special education services, even though IDEA '97 mandates that inviting the student for transition planning, including self-determination and self-advocacy, occurs at age 14. Briefly, this means getting the child and parent(s) or guardian involved in determining desires for the future and taking the necessary steps to accomplish those goals.

As further discussed below, working with the young child will imbue a sense of the idea of self-determination, focusing on preferences

Major Aspects of the IEP	
Question	**Answer**
What Is an IEP?	IEP stands for Individualized Education Program (IEP). The IEP is a written document that describes the educational plan for a student with a disability. Among other things, your IEP talks about your disability, what skills you need to learn, what you'll do in school this year, what services your school will provide, and where your learning will take place.
Why Do Students With Disabilities Need an IEP?	First, it's the law. The Individuals with Disabilities Education Act (IDEA) requires each student with disabilities who receives special education services to have an IEP – an educational program written just for him or her. Second, the IEP helps the school meet your special needs. It also helps you plan educational goals for yourself. That is why it is called an IEP – because it is an individualized education program.
What Is the Purpose of an IEP?	The purpose of the IEP is to make sure that everyone – you, members of your family, and school staff – knows what your educational program will be this year.
Where Is the IEP Developed?	The IEP is developed during an IEP meeting. The people who are concerned with your education meet, discuss, and develop your IEP goals for the next year.
Who Comes to the IEP Meeting?	Certain individuals will help write your IEP. We've listed these below. Some are required by law to come to the meeting. (In the list below, we've written these people in **bold letters.**) Others, such as you and your parents, must be invited to take part in the meeting. It's your choice to attend or not. (We've listed these people without any bolding of the letters.) All of the people listed below work together as a team to write your IEP. So – who might you see at the meeting? • You • Your parents • At least one of your **regular education** teachers, if you are (or may be) taking part in the regular education environment • At least one of your **special education teachers** (or **special education providers**) *(continued)*

Major Aspects of the IEP (continued)	
Question	**Answer**
	• **Someone who can talk about your evaluation results** and what they mean, especially what kind of instruction you need • **Someone from the school system** who knows about special education services and educating students with disabilities and who can talk about what resources the school system has – this person may be your principal, a school counselor, or someone else from the school system • People from transition service agencies (such as vocational rehabilitation), if you're going to be talking about what you plan to do after leaving high school and what you need to do now to get ready • Other people who know you – your strengths and needs – very well and who can help you plan your educational program
How Often Is the IEP Meeting Held?	The law requires that your IEP is reviewed and, if necessary, revised at least once a year. This means attending at least one IEP meeting each year. However, you, your parents, or the school can ask for more IEP meetings, if any of you think that it's necessary to take another look at your IEP.
How Long Does an IEP Meeting Last?	Approximately 30 minutes to 1 hour.
Why Should I Participate in the IEP Meeting?	It's your educational program everyone will be discussing in the meeting. Your opinions are an important part of this discussion.[1]
What Should I Do?	There are five basic steps: 1. Talk to your parents and teachers. 2. Review last year's IEP. 3. Think about your strengths and needs in school. 4. Write your goals for this school year. 5. Practice what you want to say at the meeting.

From McGahee-Kovac, M. (2002). *A student's guide to the IEP* (2nd ed). Washington, DC: National Information Center for Children and Youth with Disabilities, pp. 4-5. Reprinted with permission.
[1]In locations where student participation in the formal IEP meeting is discouraged or prohibited, meeting with team members outside of the formal setting can accomplish most of the goals of student involvement in the IEP process.

and things he or she is good at. It is this self-determination that drives a person to choose hobbies, courses, and eventual careers.

In order to be aware of a need to change a situation, and therefore need to engage in self-advocacy, a person must have sufficient awareness of self, including both strong and weak points, as well as differences from other people. Drawing a map detailing where the child is now, future goals, and what is needed to achieve those goals can be especially useful for individuals on the autism spectrum, who tend to be visually oriented. While pictures or other graphics may work well for some, text may be better for others, whereas a combination of both may suit still others. Creating lists of what works and does not work is helpful, as is listing strengths and challenges. This can help foster the development of self-determination and prepare for more structured planning regarding the IEP later on.

When helping young children determine their strengths and areas of need, it is important to remember what the child does well. For example, many young children on the autism spectrum have unusual abilities for taking apart mechanical objects, performing mathematical calculations, reading, computers, and so on. These talents, frequently connected with the child's special interests, can often be developed into courses of study in public school, higher education, and eventually careers (Grandin & Duffy, 2004).

For example, "beginning at five years of age, [I] disassembled watches using a sharp kitchen knife, removed the gears, hands, and other parts of the motor, and reassembled them. No parts were left over and the watch still worked" (Shore, 2003a, p. 59). An ability of this nature should be noticed, and the child should be made aware of the special talent. While my parents did take notice of my ability to take apart watches, I never became a watchmaker or repairer. However, that mechanical ability was later transferred to bicycles, resulting in employment through middle and high school as well as college.

In brief, starting at a young age, it is important to begin imparting to the child how a good understanding of strengths and challenges can point towards a fulfilling and productive life.

Disclosure

Disclosure is intertwined with self-advocacy. As mentioned earlier, appropriate disclosure can supply the "why" behind a request for needed accommodations. One of the three main components of the disclosure process involves a consolidation of self and examining one's own characteristics as they relate to other persons. According to Rollo May's essay *Three Worlds of Being* (1983), these three components or "worlds of being" include "the biological self," "being with myself," and "being with others."

Biological Self

The biological self (Umwelt) refers to pure biological drives, instincts, and characteristics (May, 1983). Specific examples include hair and eye color, gender, and perceptual, cognitive and affective strengths and weaknesses. Autism brings additional components to be considered, such as sensory integration issues, leading to intolerance of the humming and flickering of fluorescent lights in a classroom, for example. Other common biological domain challenges include central auditory processing disorder, scrambling verbal communications and poor motor control affecting penmanship. In a few short words, it has to do with "Who am I? Physically, cognitively, emotionally, and sensorially" (Shore, 2003b, p. 295).

Awareness of Self

The awareness of self – "being with myself" (Eigenwelt) – domain, the second domain of May's (1983) paradigm, deals with having to share with another human being one's differences from what society might consider "normal." While the primary goal for disclosure is usually to reach better mutual understanding with others, a better understanding of self often occurs in the process: "Then I finally knew why some kids were mean to me ... I was going to get the help I needed to get better grades in school and get along in life," wrote grade-school-age Ben Sawyer (2000, p. 13) as he worked through the process of disclosure. For Sawyer, this consolidation of self was a positive experience as he now had the necessary information to help himself. "Being with myself" is the world of being that, in short, deals with what my strong and weak points are and how I am going to talk to another person about them (Shore, 2003a).

Compounding the challenges of seeing oneself as different from so-called "normal" is the issue of denial. Many students have never been told about their condition, do not have complete information, or are under the misconception that by trying harder at whatever presents particular challenges, they can become just like everyone else, or "normal." Since conformity is such a strong characteristic of the public school student culture, many students vehemently deny that they have a learning difference.

Part of the difficulty in getting comfortable with disclosing autism to oneself and others is that, unlike physical disabilities, autism is "invisible." Invisible disabilities bear twin burdens. The first is greater societal stigma because people tend to believe what they see. That is, to most people those on the autism spectrum look "normal" for lack of a better word, causing speculation that poor or unusual conduct is nothing more than lax discipline on the parents' part or engagement in attention-seeking behaviors. As a result of such prevailing views, many parents hear comments such as "This child is so good-looking; there's nothing that the firm hand of discipline won't fix."

The second burden for those who have not told others of their condition is the weight of having to "pass" as normal (Goffman, 1963). In this case, others perceive the person with a difference as "normal." When circumstances dictate a disclosure, others may wonder what that person has been hiding and why it took so long for the disclosure to take place.

One way to help students grapple with this sense of difference is to look at how others with differences or disabilities have done through movies, books, and live presentations. The ideal would be to find someone with a disability who could speak to the students about what his condition means to him.

"Being with Others"

Being with others (Mitwelt or "with-world"), the third element, is more than the mere influence of others on an individual; it is the world of human interrelationships (May, 1983). According to May, more than mere adjusting and adapting in the biological sense of the Umwelt or "world around one" facet of existence, this domain implies a relationship with mutual awareness where both persons change as a result.

"Being with others" with mutual awareness can be the most difficult part of disclosure for the person on the autism spectrum. Much interpersonal interaction involves nonverbal communication such as eye contact, facial expressions and body language, which is difficult for people on the autism spectrum to process (American Psychiatric Association, 2000). "As a result, the person with autism may not be able to detect the very changes in a relationship they are trying to affect through disclosure unless the other person verbalizes in clear terms that the communication has been effective" (Shore, 2003b, p. 302). It is important for the person on the autism spectrum to request verbal feedback from the other person during the disclosure process. For example, "Now that we have discussed how autism affects my testing performance, do you have any further questions that can lead to a better understanding of my situation?"

In a school setting, "being with others" means being aware of how the student consciously interprets fellow students' reactions to a disclosure and other behaviors as well. For example, if Roberta tells Keisha that she has Asperger Syndrome causing Keisha to respond "Asparagus Syndrome?," how does that make Roberta feel? Will Roberta be able to accurately decode Keisha's reaction of surprise, mocking, or other emotion? This "world" is not merely a matter of how Keisha feels about Roberta, but rather how Roberta interprets Keisha's reaction to her. Hopefully, Roberta's interpretation of Keisha's response is relevant to how Keisha feels. In the student-teacher relational domain, the question becomes "how do I determine how the new math teacher feels when I tell her I find several problems on a single worksheet visually overwhelming?"

Ruth Elaine Hane's discussion in Chapter 1 of reading and transmitting nonverbal cues by organizing the face and body into geometric shapes provides the structure many people on the autism spectrum need to begin working on this challenging area of communication.

The following worksheet, based on Rollo May's *Three Worlds of Being*, may be helpful to students in sorting out the "three worlds of being" issues when considering disclosure to a fellow student, teacher, or other person about being on the autism spectrum.

For example, suppose a student felt a need to tell his writing teacher why he does so well on take-home writing assignments that are prepared on a computer but so poorly on the in-class creative writing projects that have to be written by hand. Possibly with help from a trusted teacher or guidance counselor, the student can sort out and think through some key areas while considering his disclosure. It is often fairly easy to work out one's strengths and challenges as well as how to describe them, but figuring out how to interpret the writing teacher's response may be more difficult. It helps to obtain direct feedback from the writing teacher rather than rely on nonverbal and other subtle cues indicating the teacher's response. Thus, the student may just simply ask, "does what I say make sense to you?"

The Three Worlds of Being as Related to Disclosure

Biological Self	
What are my strengths and challenges?	

With Myself	
How am I going to talk about these challenges?	

With Others	
How can I interpret the other person's reactions to my discussion?	

Adapted from Shore, S. (2003b). Disclosure for people on the autism spectrum. In L. Willey (Ed.), *Asperger syndrome in adolescence: Living with the ups, the downs, and things in between.* London: Jessica Kingsley Publishing, p. 306. Reprinted with permission.

The Individualized Education Program

The public schools are mandated by the Individuals with Disabilities and Education Act (IDEA) to provide a customized free and appropriate public education to students needing special education services. Following assessment and diagnosis, the lynchpin for determining and enabling these special education services is the IEP.

The beauty of using the IEP as a tool for building skills in self-advocacy and disclosure is that it already exists. Presently, the IEP involves different professionals and parents meeting to create a customized education for the child. Even though IDEA '97 states "The public agency shall ensure that the IEP team for each child includes, if appropriate, the child" (34 C.F.R. §300.344(a)(7), in reality, the child is often left out of this process until the federally mandated age of 14 when plans for transitioning out of the public school must be written into the IEP.

A fundamental flaw in this design is that the student is marginalized to one of the petals of the diagram shown on page 77. Instead, the student should be placed in the center since the whole reason for an IEP is to create the best possible education for the child. The individual student best knows his or her strengths and challenges within the educational experience, and having this intimate knowledge places the student in a unique position to advocate for the necessary accommodations. Moreover, playing an integral part in designing his or her education prepares the student for a fulfilling and productive life in society by learning early on the skill of self-advocacy and appropriate disclosure. The self-initiated IEP is one answer to developing this skill.

The Self-Initiated Individual Education Plan

As indicated in the graphic on page 78, using the self-initiated IEP, the child is no longer included in the IEP *as appropriate,* but is included *as appropriate to his or her ability* (Field, 1996). No changes of design or implementation of the IEP are needed. What is needed is a way to imbue sufficient knowledge to students to allow them to participate actively in IEP development and meetings, and in doing so develop skills in self-advocacy. The self-initiated IEP is one where students take a central role in advocating for their needs and developing their education according to their needs (McGahee, Mason, Wallace, & Jones, 2001), thus aiding in developing a sense of self-determination.

Special attention to developing a sense of self-determination for students with disabilities is critical to help ameliorate the adult assistance typically received in the public schools and elsewhere. This adult assistance can result in an overreliance on other people's opinions for decisions that should be made for oneself. The self-initiated IEP aids in teaching those with disabilities "to act as the primary causal agent in one's life and making choices and decisions regarding one's quality of life free from undue external influence or interference" (Wehmeyer, 1996, p. 24).

The ultimate goal for students' involvement in their own IEP is that by middle or high school they are leading their own IEP meeting under the watchful eye of the IEP team.

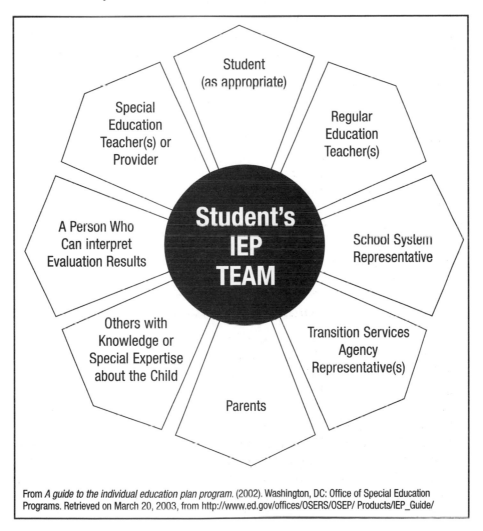

From *A guide to the individual education plan program*. (2002). Washington, DC: Office of Special Education Programs. Retrieved on March 20, 2003, from http://www.ed.gov/offices/OSERS/OSEP/ Products/IEP_Guide/

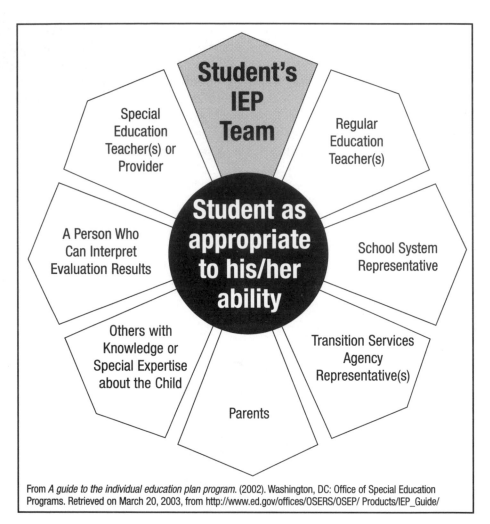

From *A guide to the individual education plan program*. (2002). Washington, DC: Office of Special Education Programs. Retrieved on March 20, 2003, from http://www.ed.gov/offices/OSERS/OSEP/ Products/IEP_Guide/

Case of Frankie D'Erasmo

Frankie, soon to graduate from high school, has, with much support from his parents, Sandy and Frank, been very successful in directing the research, planning, and discussion of his IEP. In doing so, Frankie benefits in a number of ways. First, he has worked through the issues of self-disclosure and then disclosed to other people that he is on the autism spectrum. Second, he is well equipped to understand how Asperger Syndrome affects him in various areas of his life and what he can do about it. Third, he has practiced talking about his needs and how to obtain reasonable accommodations in a way that others can easily understand, as illustrated in the following.

To advocate for yourself in an IEP meeting sounds like a daunting task. But from past experiences, it isn't all that bad. IEP meetings have set dates, usually in the first quarter of the school year, but there's no particular need to prepare for them as a student. Defining an IEP meeting in my terms is basically a place to lay out your plans for the future on and off campus. The meetings I took part in usually lasted about 45 minutes. I'll go ahead and describe an IEP meeting I had in the past.

The people present at the meetings are usually familiar faces: my homeroom teacher and teacher assistant, my mom, and my social worker. There's also two people from my county: a secretary that types down everything that goes on and a board member that mostly runs the meeting.

For the most part, everyone besides myself did the talking. A small bit of it wasn't of importance to me, but most of the topics deserved my attention (it's about me, after all!). It's important to demonstrate good listening, because while I didn't have to speak too much, it was important to listen in. Two topics that particularly got my attention are the pros and cons of my current schoolwork and myself in general. They discussed my IEP goals, most of them on social skills. They pointed out my weaknesses in any classes and my strong points as well. My extracurricular activities and hobbies were also discussed.

Next, they would go over my state requirements. In Maryland [where I live], it is required that students do at least 75 hours of volunteer work (no pay) and pass a group of tests called the Maryland Functional Tests. There's also the High School Assessment Tests, but I just have to take those without having to pass.

Around this point, some of the attendants would pass around a couple of papers that require signatures. It wasn't necessary to look over the papers before signing; they were of no particular importance to me except for signing, of course.

Next, are my future plans. They described what colleges I'm considering, what jobs I'm interested in, and so forth. This doesn't take too long and after that, the meeting began to wind down. Before the end of the meeting, the secretary that is keeping the notes would summarize what everyone discussed. The board member would ask if there's any more questions and then adjourn the meeting.

My mother received copies of various papers showing my IEP goals, old report cards, my credits, etc. The first two papers were the most important as they summarized the meeting. They included my overall adjustment to the school, an academic narrative, a clinical nar-

rative, and recommendations from my teachers. Essentially, these papers are like my blueprints.

I'm sure that IEP meetings will vary from school to school. The two most important things a student should do are to listen as much as you can and speak when you can. The main focus of these meetings is about the student, so it's important that the student give his or her input. Don't be afraid to ask questions. If you missed or forgot anything about the IEP meeting, you will receive papers that summarize the meeting. Feel free to look those over.

While these meetings do center around the student, there's no need to worry. I treat them as I would a normal meeting: stay quiet unless spoken to, and give comments. (Frankie D'Erasmo, personal communication, February 8, 2004)

Ways to Get Students Involved

Many students will not be able to initiate the same kind of advanced planning as Frankie. The goal is to provide similar experiences to the best of the child's ability. For example, a 4-year-old in preschool cannot be expected to undergo the introspection, planning, and verbal interaction necessary to lead her own IEP. However, there are still ways for her to get involved. Perhaps the most this child can do is to come into the IEP meeting, help hand out some materials and then leave.

To my IEP team,

I like the way Mr. Dowd teaches math. He makes it fun and easy for me. Mrs. Sugarman's English class is very difficult. I don't understand when she diagrams sentences on the board and the scratching of the student pencils during writing time makes it very hard for me to concentrate.

Truly yours,
Joey

Another child may be able to read two or three prepared sentences such as, "When Mr. Dowd teaches math, I find it confusing. When Mrs. Sugarman teaches grammar, I find that easy." Other children may be able to go more into detail about why certain courses or subjects are difficult or easy and/or talk about environmental challenges.

Not all involvement has to be verbal. Other means of communication can be used, ranging from writing or typing a letter to using a DynaVox™. About the size of a notebook computer, the DynaVox™ enables the user to select graphics in order to communicate via synthesized voice. Those graphics can be selected several ways such as via a touch screen, mouse-compatible pointing device, or a switch joystick.

If the student is unable to physically attend the IEP meeting, a letter, a tape recording, or perhaps a conversation through a speaker phone are other ways of participating in the IEP process consistent with the requirement that, "If the student does not attend the IEP meeting, the public agency shall take other steps to ensure the student's preferences and interests are considered" (34 C.F.R. §300.344(b)(2).

The most successful people are those who are aware of their strengths and challenges. Having a strong sense of internal locus of control, these people view themselves as a major influence in determining their destiny, thereby increasing their self-efficacy. According to Bandura (1986), people with a high degree of self-efficacy are able to link cognitive, social, and behavioral skills into an integrated course of action for dealing with their environment. This contrasts with those who have an external locus of control, who believe that their fate lies in preordered events and other people's whims.

Giving students personal responsibility in developing the IEP rather than being passive participants in their education makes their educational experience more meaningful, and is reflected in higher achievement later in life (deCharms, 1976, 1992) due to a heightened sense of self-determination. Additionally, the greater involvement in one's own IEP leads to more ability to successfully advocate and disclose as needed.

Public School Responsibilities

The public schools are charged with preparing the nation's youth to lead fulfilling and productive lives according to the customs of a child's society. For most, that involves the mastery of reading, writing, arithmetic, civic awareness and other content areas, as well as a sense of responsibility and moral development. On the other hand, self-advocacy and disclosure are not given serious consideration, as evidenced by a large number of students with disabilities who graduate high school lacking sufficient understanding of their disabilities and how certain accommodations can help maximize their strengths and enhance their lives (Hughes & Carter, 2000). For students with special needs, and in particular those on the autism spectrum, self-advocacy and disclosure must be taught just like other content areas.

Children with special needs often suffer from a diminished sense of self-efficacy or a reduced "belief in one's capabilities to organize and execute the course of action required to manage prospective situations" (Bandura, 1995, p. 2). As described in Kassiane Sibley's six-step method of developing skills in self-advocacy in Chapter 2, increasing a person's self-efficacy in this area requires enactive mastery, or performance accomplishment (deCharms, 1972). Also critical are vicarious experiences through modeling, verbal persuasion through exhortation, and physiological states from emotional arousal (Bandura, 1997), such as working through an anxiety-producing challenge to feel the elation of success upon completion. An important benefit of attaining skill in self-advocacy and disclosure is an improved internal locus of control, which means that the person perceives his or her destiny as being under his or her own control (Lefcourt, 1982).

Implementing the Self-Initiated IEP in a School Setting

There are five phases that teachers may want to consider as they plan for meaningful inclusion of students in their own IEP. The first step involves planning what must be done to set the stage before involving the students. Once everything is in place, students should first be made aware of, and then learn to understand, their IEP, particularly how it relates to them. With such understanding, students can move on to participating in the IEP team meeting to the fullest extent of their ability, including writing their IEP. Finally, teachers will want to encourage and monitor continued and appropriate student self-advocacy both within and outside of the strict confines of the IEP.

Setting the Stage

Administrative support from department chair(s), principal(s), special education director(s), and others in supervisory positions within the school is vital before teachers even start the process. These individuals will want to know the why, who, and how much (in terms of time, and often money) is required to implement the process. Administrators and others are often more open to the idea of the self-initiated IEP if the initial proposal is presented as a pilot study to be expanded if successful (McGahee et al., 2001).

As part of being more directly involved in developing and implementing their IEP, students will need to look at their own and possibly other IEPs as examples. When preparing to develop a self-initiated IEP program, therefore, teachers must determine and follow school policies on where such documents are located, confidentiality practices, procedures for students viewing their own IEP, making copies, and safe return of the documents. The increased circulation of IEP materials also makes it important to take steps to minimize the risk of inappropriate disclosure of private information as well as follow school and/or district policies when working with these documents. A totally fictional IEP created to avoid the remote possibility of an IEP being identified with a particular student is sometimes ideal.

Selecting Students

Once the procedural and administrative hurdles have been overcome, it is important for two reasons to consider which student(s) have the greatest likelihood of being successful at becoming actively involved in their own IEP. First, involving students in their IEP may be a new area for the teacher, so it is important to become familiar with what is entailed by starting out with a student who is capable and eager to learn before attempting more challenging situations. Second, successes with the first student(s) provide encouragement for others to participate later on, and is also more convincing to administrators and others whose support is critical. Therefore, it is recommended to start by choosing students who are well liked, do well academically, have a clear sense of interests, and are motivated to be included in determining their own destiny.

The students chosen should have sufficient time in their schedule to meet with their teacher(s) and to work on their IEP. Likely candidates are students who are two to three months away from the next annual IEP review, as this provides ample time for them to learn about and prepare their IEP while maintaining a short enough time frame to make the work meaningful to them. Further, parental or guardian support is needed along with reassurance that the rights and confidentiality of the child will not be violated.

Student involvement is supported by IDEA '97. The challenge is to implement this involvement via the self-initiated IEP.

Teaching Students About the IEP

As with any other school subject, when teaching students how to become involved with their IEP, it is vital to determine instructional goals and objectives while keeping in mind that the endpoint is for students to further their self-advocacy skills. Enabling students to think about the future will improve their ability to regulate planning and behavior now (Bandura, 1986). To that end, teachers may ask questions such as, "What will the student be able to do as a result of this education?" "What will the student be able to do in the next month or months? End of the year? End of several years?"

Just as when transitioning to any other new activity, prepare the student in advance of the IEP meeting and describe its purpose. Student involvement can take place on a sliding scale of responsibility. Initially, and/or for students at a lower cognitive or developmental stage, having students just be familiar with the purpose of an IEP can be sufficient and all that can reasonably be expected. The range of involvement might include the following:

- The teacher brings the student to the IEP meeting for a brief period of time, encouraging interaction with some or all the team members. This introduction may be as short as a few minutes where the student just says "hi" to one or two IEP team members or helps pass out materials.

- The student prepares a short statement that he or she distributes or reads aloud to the IEP team indicating strengths and difficulties in school.

- After obtaining data from IEP team members prior to the meeting, the student writes sections of the IEP for modification and approval at the IEP meeting.

- The student co-presents as an equal member of the IEP team.

- The student leads the IEP meeting with support from his or her primary teacher.

Additional goals and objects should be planned for transition by the IDEA '97-mandated age of 14. As mentioned, it is important to adjust these goals as needed to match the ability of the child.

Again, just as with every other subject, it is important to develop a lesson plan and anticipate questions and concerns that students may have as they work on applying their strengths and challenges to creating their own customized education. For example, teachers must explain why a student was given a certain diagnosis and by whom. The discussion of the diagnosis should include strengths and needs as applied to the particular student both in and out of school, making the diagnosis a shorthand way of explaining a condition rather than a label. In this context, it is important to check how the district handles disclosure of test score results that led the clinician to make a given diagnosis. The present level of educational performance area can be used to facilitate discussion for strategizing to improve grades. Other areas of the IEP that merit discussion include goals, medical needs, and accommodations.

Honesty is vital, because students can usually detect when teachers are not being forthright with them. Remaining honest, yet tactful, also provides a valuable role model for the students to be honest with themselves as they plan how to use their abilities and strengths to accommodate for their challenges.

It is important to schedule sufficient time for students to develop the necessary knowledge and skills to take a lead in putting together a customized education that they are entitled to under IDEA '97. In that connection, the teacher should consider which aspects of the IEP can be taught through group instruction and which areas require individual attention.

Preparing for administrative support, addressing confidentiality, determining which students to start with, obtaining parental support, drawing out goals and objectives, dealing with the issues of disclosure, and being able to talk the students through the sections of the IEP, all of these areas lay the groundwork for actual student participation in the process.

Introducing Students to Their IEP

Some students may be able to relate the contents of their IEP to their education almost right away. Others may be aware that they have an IEP but have no clear idea of its function, still others may not know that they have an IEP at all. Prior to educating students about the IEP, teachers must determine the extent of students' knowledge of the IEP and the IEP process through conversation or a written survey to match their instructional efforts to students' learning styles and abilities.

To maximize learning involvement and understanding, addressing individual situations will help students relate to their own IEP. For example, a student who indicates that borrowing notes from a classmate helps to learn course material can translate this into a recommended accommodation that involves providing the student access to notes from other classmates or possibly the teacher.

The following questions, developed by the National Information Center for Children and Youth with Disabilities (2002), asked either in discussion or written format, may be helpful at this stage.

- How do you learn best? What type of lesson really helps you learn? (For example, you like to read new information or hear it first, or you prefer to work in small groups or alone . . .)

- What is a disability?

- Do you have a disability?

- There is a law that allows you to receive special services from the school. What's the name of the law?

- What is accommodation?

- Do you have any accommodations in your classes?

- What's an IEP?

- Do you have an IEP?

From National Information Center for Children and Youth with Disabilities. (2002). *Technical assistance guide: Helping students develop their IEPs.* Washington, DC: Author, p. 5. Reprinted with permission.

Familiarity with the looks, purpose, rationale, and the various sections of the IEP is necessary for students to gain a foundational understanding of this document. Some students may only be able to grasp the uses for and different parts of the IEP. Others may be interested in the history and the legal aspects of the document as well.

As an introduction to the document, giving them a copy of their own IEP, the teacher guides students through the key sections. A worksheet similar to the one presented on the following pages can help structure the process via group or individual discussion. Particular situations may require the addition, modification, or subtraction of some of the questions.

This worksheet will help bring meaning to and engage students in their IEP. More advanced students can use the worksheet to help in their own assessment of their current IEP and to prepare for the upcoming IEP meeting.

My Individualized Education Plan	
Name _____ Date _____	

Question	Answer
Where is my name located?	
When is the date of my next review?	
What does the "present level of educational performance" tell me?	
What are my measurable annual goals?	
Are there any short-term objectives and what do they say?	
What special education and related services am I provided?	
Why was I given these services?	
What supplementary aids and services are provided?	
What are they used for?	
What program modification(s) were made?	
For what reason(s)?	

My Individualized Education Plan (continued)	
Question	**Answer**
When are the time(s) that I will spend time in a resource or special room?	
For what reason(s)?	
What accommodations are needed for me to take the state or district assessment?	
If I take an alternate assessment, what will that look like?	
How will my progress toward annual goals be measured?	
How will my parents and I be informed of my progress towards these annual goals?	
What steps am I taking to prepare for life after graduation?	
What right(s) will be transferred to me upon reaching the age of majority?	

Note. Transition services are usually not considered until age 14. However, in keeping with the philosophy of using the IEP as a tool for building skills in self-advocacy and disclosure, it is never too early to start planning for the transition into post-public school life. In fact, the teacher will want to introduce the topic by talking about how the IEP is also used for planning the future. Questions such as "What would you like to do when you graduate school?" can get the ball rolling on transition at a very early age.

Probing Further into the IEP

After students have become familiar with the look, feel, and ultimate purpose of their IEP, assessing and updating the document itself can begin. Going section by section, have students restate in their own words what is written in their IEP, followed by making comments about and suggesting changes that will help them assume ownership of the process. Below are suggestions for helping students work through the many sections of the IEP (McGahee et al., 2001).

Goals
- Subject by subject, list the students' strengths and needs. Sometimes a worksheet helps. Structuring the review with symbols can also help. For example, a check mark next to a goal indicates the student feels that that goal has been achieved. A question mark indicates not meeting that goal. Encourage students to write their own goals as they see fit.
- Find out what enabled students to meet their goals (or prevented them from doing so). In doing so, consider asking students who seem "stuck" to consider test scores, project completion, and other definable products.
- Encourage students to ask their subject teachers, parents, and other appropriate people for their opinions on whether goals have been met, and what would be helpful in the future for the student to meet these goals if they have not been achieved, or what might make meeting the goal easier.

Statement of the Special Education and Related Services and Supplementary Aids and Services to Be Provided to the Child
- Find out what students know related to accommodations. Can they describe some accommodations that were useful to them? What accommodations, if any, were not helpful?
- Ask students to talk about what made their best class so good. Was it the way the teacher presented the subject? Was there something about the homework assignments? Is there anything about the physical classroom environment that could be improved? Similarly, classes where the student did not do so well should be discussed.
- Have students ask their subject area teachers for their opinions of their strengths and needs.
- Using an accommodations menu like the one on page 91, have students first check off the accommodations that are currently being used for each class. After rating the usefulness of each accommodation, the student can then recommend useful modifications to the list. It is important to concentrate on the most useful accommodations rather than a large number of different accommodation.

Transition out of School

Although thinking about transition for children with special needs is often delayed until the federally mandated age of 14, relating accommodations to life outside of school as early as possible can serve as an important stepping stone to success after graduation. After determining the students' interests through specific discussions of interests and where students see themselves working when they get out of school, have students look at how their present accommodations can relate to their life after graduation. For example, a student with Asperger Syndrome may have accommodations for aural and visual sensitivities in school. Several questions may be asked about these and other school-based accommodations. How will the student determine if the accommodations are needed after graduation? How will requests for such accommodations be made? Perhaps even more important, what suggestions for accommodations can be made along with the request so that a solution is presented simultaneously?

Whereas the public schools are responsible for devising appropriate accommodations during the school years, after graduation most of this responsibility shifts to the person making the request. For example, a student's poor motor control and depth perception may preclude driving a car. As a result, alternate modes of transportation must be considered. Have students meet with a representative or employee from one of the agencies that deal with these and other challenges the student will face in the adult world, such as Vocational Rehabilitation. Within this context, also discuss with students their ideas of where they see themselves in different aspects of adult life, including goals and objectives that lead toward their preferences in these areas.

Further research into adult life as appropriate can be done in the form of job shadowing, participation in vocational programs and review of admission requirements for colleges as well as their disability offices. Ideally, students' responsibility for their own IEP should steadily increase to the point that they can take the lead in developing this document by the time they graduate. The more a student can do while still in school, the more capable he will be in developing and maintaining his own "Individualized Life Plan" with the benefits for self-determination and success that go along with it. The form on page 92 helps initiate and guide thinking in this area.

However, students should not feel that they are pressured into making binding commitments for their adult lives. Instead, the focus should be on discussing and planning how students think they would like their

Accommodations Menu

Note: This form is not required by IDEA

Student: _____ Date: _____

Teacher: _____ IEP Manager: _____

Used ?	Effective-ness (1-5)	Accommodation	Used ?	Effective-ness (1-5)	Accommodation

		Placement
		Preferential seating
		Small group
					Sensory
					Lighting modifications
					Hat with visor
					Different-color paper
					Headphones
					Chewing gum
					Standing at desk
					Sitting on therapy ball
					Small therapy ball or other
					   manipulative for hands
					Quiet (safe) room for dealing
					   with sensory overload

		Assignments Reduced level of difficulty Shortened assignments Reduced pencil/paper tasks Extended time Opportunity to respond orally			

		Instruction
		Shortened instruction
		Assignment notebook
		Frequent/immediate feedback
		Dictated information,
		   answers on tape
		Taped lectures
		Reduced language level/
		   reading style
		Incorporation of learning styles.
		Peer tutoring/paired working
		   arrangement
		Outline with due dates for
		   assignments/tests
		Negotiated respite with teacher
		   (medical)
		Restroom use (medical)
					Materials and technology
					Taped text/material
					Highlighted text/materials
					Manipulatives
					Braille materials
					ESL materials
					Calculator
					Keyboard modifications
					Access to keyboard/word
					   processor
					Large print
					Using tape recorder in classroom
					Using another student's notes
					Using teacher's notes
					Having note-taker in class
					Extra set of books for home
					   (physical)
					Electronic speller

		Behavior Positive reinforcement Frequent breaks Clearly defined limits/ expectations Quiet time Behavior management plan			**Teacher Supports** Consultation Information Other
		Testing Scheduling Setting Presentation Response Extended time Individual/small-group testing Take test in quiet area Test read orally Take test orally Dictate answers to a test/quiz Use calculator on test/quiz Open-book exams			**Other** _____ _____ _____ _____ _____ _____
			Notes	_____ _____ _____ _____	

Adapted from *Student-led IEPs. A guide for student involvement* by McGahee et al. (p.23). Copyright 2001 by the Council for Exceptional Children. Reprinted with permission.

life to be after graduation and how they are going to satisfy these preferences. Meaningful work on planning transition for life out of school is great practice for becoming one's own "case manager," as discussed in detail in Roger Meyer's chapter, "Being Your Own Case Manager."

MY ADULT LIFE	
Student: _____ Date: _____	
Employment	
Goals	
Current Accommodations	
Future Accommodations	
Recreation and Leisure	
Goals	
Current Accommodations	
Future Accommodations	
Home/Independent Living	
Goals	
Current Accommodations	
Future Accommodations	
Community Involvement/Volunteer Work	
Goals	
Current Accommodations	
Future Accommodations	
Postsecondary Education/Training	
Goals	
Current Accommodations	
Future Accommodations	

The Actual Writing of the IEP

As mentioned previously, students vary in their ability to assess, plan, and write their own IEP. Some students may be able to complete one or more sections on their own, whereas others may be able to talk about or otherwise communicate their needs with teachers or others doing the writing. Still other students many need prompting. A possible sequence adapted from McGahee and colleagues (2001) for preparing the IEP follows.

- Ask students to describe their disabilities in terms of their effect on life at home, school, and the community.

  – What about the disability makes things harder?
  Ex: "My motor control challenges make it difficult for me to be successful in team-oriented sports in gym class."

  – Is there anything that strengths from your disability make easier?
  Ex: "When Mr. Roberts diagrams sentence structure on the board, it is easier for me to understand because of my strong visual skills."

  – What should others know about your disability?
  Ex: "Teachers need to know that my central-auditory processing disorder makes it difficult for me to learn from a lecture mode of teaching. Providing me with notes before class helps keep me on track."

- Have students determine whether they have met current goals and objectives as well as develop new ones, being mindful of what is realistic.

- Go over and write down strengths and needs for each class.
  Ex: "Geometry is easy because it's easy for me to visualize the shapes used."

- Review the accommodations needs checklist on page 91 to identify examples and ideas for accommodations needed for each class. It is important to stress that accommodations are for "leveling the playing field" rather than providing an unfair advantage.
  Ex: "Having access to an AlphaSmart™ or some other keyboarding device allows me to concentrate on my writing because I don't have to spend so much energy making sure that my handwriting is legible."

- Some students may be able to talk directly about their behavioral and social strengths and needs. Others may need a checklist similar to the one below to work out goals and accommodations in this area. Have students enlist the help of their parents and general education teachers in preparing the worksheet below.

	BEHAVIORAL AND SOCIAL STRENGTHS AND NEEDS CHECKLIST	
✓	Item	Suggestion for Improvement (If Needed)
	I am usually on time.	Carry a schedule and refer to it frequently. Save reading posters in the hallways for before and after school.
	I talk to my peers outside of school.	Call one friend from school on Mondays, Wednesdays, and Saturdays.
	I sit by myself on the bus to and from school.	Arrange to sit next to a friend in school before the bus ride home.

- Have students match up and describe the needed accommodations to succeed with their classroom goals. Discussion about responsibilities that students have to take on as well as their plans for the next year and after graduation is important in order to maintain a long-range view toward leading their own IEP and, eventually, their lives after graduation.

- Have students start preparing drafts of the section(s) of their IEP they want to work on. Encourage students to share their work with parents, teachers and other appropriate persons. Allocate sufficient time for teacher review and feedback during this step. It is helpful to ask students to read their own IEP as if they were the teacher, or to ask questions such as "Can you explain why this accommodation will help you" in a role-playing mode.

Preparing for the IEP Meeting

While many schools follow the recommendations of IDEA '97 with regard to student attendance at IEP meetings, much more can be done to encourage meaningful involvement in terms of preparing for and participating in their IEP meeting. Again, there are different levels of participation for the student attending IEP meetings, ranging from least to most, as suggested in the following.

1. Help pass out materials to other members and possibly stay for a little while afterwards.

2. Deliver verbally, or by other means, a short prepared statement on easy and difficult areas of school. The student may stay on afterwards and even answer questions or engage in other appropriate dialogue to the best of her ability. Initially, some students may find it difficult to verbally explain their situation and needs to the IEP team. See Liane Willey's chapter on "Disclosure and Self-Advocacy: An Open Door Policy" for ideas on how to present this information in writing through agents.

The next levels of participation treat the student as a full member of the IEP team.

3. The student stays for part of the meeting and dialogues with the IEP team leader and other members of the IEP team.

4. The student stays for the entire meeting and dialogues with the IEP team leader and other members of the IEP team.

5. The student co-presents with the IEP team leader, providing information about himself for inclusion in the IEP. There should be agreement between the IEP team leader and the student beforehand regarding their specific responsibilities.

6. The student leads the IEP throughout the meeting, taking on the responsibilities of welcoming, introducing, orienting team members to the agenda, and directing the conversation *under the watchful eye of the person who would otherwise have been the team leader.*

Planning for Success

Just as with any other meeting, proper planning and organization are necessary for success. In fact, the steps the student takes in preparing to lead his or her own IEP meeting are similar to what any other team member would do to prepare.

First and foremost, students must be familiar with their IEP, or at least the section(s) they plan to present on. The following suggestions for familiarizing the student with the IEP have been adapted from McGahee et al. (2001, pp. 28-29).

1. Prime students in preparing for their IEP meeting by having them think about their role in the IEP meeting:
   "What would you want members in the IEP meeting to know?"
   "Which part(s) of the IEP do you wish to present?"
   As much as possible, serve as a consultant as students construct their presentation. The ideal is to send the message that "it's my job to make possible what you want to happen" – within reason, of course.

2. Suggest and provide presentation prompts such as:
   • Script or notes on paper or numbered index cards (numbering makes it easier to put the cards back in order in case they are dropped)
   • Highlighters
   • Powerpoint presentation

3. Work with the student on the skills of:
   • Listening
   • Speaking clearly
   • Using PowerPoint software
   • Asking questions
   • Stating disagreements appropriately
   • Taking notes

4. Role-play different scenarios.

5. Provide instruction in the following areas as needed in the protocol of a typical IEP meeting. Individual components are determined by the extent to which students will be involved in the IEP meeting:
   • Greeting people as they enter the meeting room
   • Making introductions (students who are uncomfortable making introductions or do not know all the people present can ask that the team members introduce themselves)

- Reviewing the agenda
- Explaining legal requirements
- Asking for questions and feedback as well as listening and processing of feedback
- Sticking to the agenda
- Keeping track of time
- Closing the meeting by summarizing decisions and thanking everyone

Although official notification of an IEP meeting and agenda has to be initiated by the IEP team leader, students should be encouraged to prepare and send their own invitation and agenda for the meeting as well. Such involvement helps further prepare students for the meeting. At the same time, the special invitation prepares IEP team members for a meeting where the student will play a significant role. Similar to the "official" meeting notification, the students' version should include the date, location, and topics to be covered. A place should also be provided for team member feedback to be returned in cases where team members are unable to attend the meeting.

Inviting the members of the IEP team in this manner lays the groundwork for building allies both within the school environment and beyond. Creating allies furthers a person's self-advocacy efforts because it aligns the student for greater community building and support. (Read more about the importance of allies in Phil Schwarz's chapter, "Building Alliances: Community Identity and the Role of Allies in Autistic Self-Advocacy.")

Many IEP team meetings consist of the members talking about and planning for a student's customized education program. The challenge will be to continue this planning but with the student in the room as an active and equally valued member of the team. It is important for team members to make sure that the student feels included. Some ways of ensuring this is achieved include the following table, adapted from McGahee et al. (2001, p. 31).

Ways to Make Students Feel Included	
Tip	**Reason**
Look at the student when he or she is talking. Note: You many want to just look in the student's general direction if he or she is averse to eye contact.	Shows you are listening.
Use the student's name when speaking to him or her.	Creates a sense of belonging.
Direct comments about the student directly to the student instead of referring to him or her in the third person.	Demonstrates team members' awareness of the presence of the student.
Ask for the student's input and thoughts before asking the other members of the team.	Emphasizes the importance of the student's input.
Allow ample time for the student to finish speaking before commenting.	It may take the student more time than a typical person to communicate verbally or otherwise.
Restate what the student says in your own words.	Lets student know you were listening and ensures your understanding of what he or she means.
Ask the student at regular intervals if he or she has any questions.	Ensures student understanding of events at the meeting.
Make sure other team members are aware of the student's neurocognitive and/or sensory challenges.	Allows for accommodation of possible unexpected student responses or questions.
Make sure the student knows he or she can take a break or leave if needed.	Minimizes student stress and helps student feel safe in what can be an emotionally challenging event.

Supporting the Student at the IEP Meeting

Below are supportive actions that can be taken at the IEP meeting to help ensure success, as adapted from *Student-Led IEPs. A Guide for Student Involvement* (McGahee et al., 2001, p. 32).

1. Have someone serve as a secretary to alleviate the pressure and distractions of having to take notes as well as work with the student as team leader.

2. Be prepared to allow additional time for explanations and translating between the student and the other team members.

3. A presentation at a meeting is a performance, so the student may be nervous. The supportive teacher will do the following to ensure the student feels as safe as possible:

   • Acknowledge the time and effort the student has spent preparing for the meeting.
   • Prepare a backup plan with the student in case he or she becomes overwhelmed or an unexpected discussion of an event causes excess anxiety. The student will feel much better knowing that a backup plan is ready if needed.

After the meeting, discuss the student's reactions to the meeting and use them as a springboard for preparing for the next IEP meeting. Employing the ideas and procedures presented in this and other chapters in this book has most likely taught the student much in working with his or her strengths and challenges to create a customized education according to his or her need. These vital skills in self-advocacy and disclosure can be generalized for the next IEP meeting and, more important, life after graduation.

Generalizing to the College Level

One of the major challenges in presenting the need for accommodations at all educational levels, as well as in the workplace, is to structure the request in a way that is understandable to the person we are asking to do the modifications. An accommodations worksheet like the sample on page 100 can be very helpful in working out needed accommodations.

Accommodations Worksheet

Name: _____ Any Student _____
School: _____ Any State College _____
Counselor: _____ Unnamed Somebody _____
Date: _____ August 15, 2006 _____

Challenge	Cause	Suggested Accommodation
Taking tests with multiple questions per page.	Visually overstimulating; gets lost in all the words.	1. Only one question per page. 2. Two sheets of paper to cover distracting verbiage.
Unable to concentrate with fluorescent lights on.	Visual sensitivity results in perceiving the 60Hz cycling of the lights.	Explore alternate lighting, sit next to window, wear baseball cap in class.
Classroom too noisy to take exams.	Central auditory processing disorder (scrambles sensory input).	Separate testing room. Make sure the room has a nonfluorescent lighting source (see above).
Scheduling long-term assignments.	Poor executive function.	Regularly meet with professor (perhaps once a week) to keep on target with lengthy assignments.

One college student I advocated for had difficulties obtaining the necessary classroom and academic accommodations. Even the thought of going to the university disabilities office was very stressful for the student due to past failure in getting anyone to understand what accommodations she needed. Like many with Asperger Syndrome, this student has a high IQ and is very capable in several areas but needs help in others. As for the self-initiated IEP, preparation before going to the disability office counselor was needed.

First, making the initial appointment with the counselor proved to be a challenge because a person rarely answered the phone at the disability counselor's office and voice messages left were not returned. Initially, I wondered if the student was using this as an excuse to avoid an unpleasant situation, so I tried myself. The college web site failed to provide e-mail addresses of persons who could be contacted to make an appointment. After many phone calls, I finally reached a live person and made an appointment three weeks into the future. In the meantime, I met with the student to draw up a plan, including how to deal with a disability counselor who might know very little about Asperger Syndrome and even less about devising appropriate accommodations.

The day prior to the meeting I met with the student for a final preparation for our meeting with the counselor. This meant filling out the accommodations worksheet to help the student organize her thoughts and generate notes to rely on when talking with the counselor. Working through the worksheet was very difficult for her. Several times during the process the student would shut down, become nonverbal and even start head banging. One time, she stood up and walked in tight circles, unable to talk or otherwise communicate. When communication was possible, we talked through the challenges the student faced in attending school and specific classes.

Calling the difficulties "challenges" rather than "problems" seemed to make it easier for her to look for solutions. Some of the challenges faced by the student as a result of her Asperger Syndrome included making sense of the teacher's lectures, becoming visually overwhelmed by busy assignment sheets and tests, getting overwhelmed by fluorescent lights, managing long-term assignments, as well as just realizing when things were going wrong.

With much trepidation on the student's part, we met the disabilities counselor the next day. As I began introducing myself as the student's advocate, the counselor indicated that she knew who I was from an article written about me in *Intervention in School and Clinic* that she had in her desk drawer. Because we were well organized, the counselor was very receptive to the student's needs and even came up with some helpful hints on her own. One of these suggestions was to allow the student to still be considered full-time even after being reduced to a 75% course load. The following gives a glimpse of the student's experience in her own words.

> *The thought of asking for accommodations was overwhelming to me. Academic work is no problem – except when I get bored. And accommodations are for students who can't do the work, right? Admitting that I needed accommodations felt like admitting weakness when, in fact, my problems are caused by difference.*

> *My main problems are an inability to follow through with long-term assignments and sensory sensitivities that make it difficult for me to focus in the classroom. This is not stuff that shows up on a test, and in the past I've run into variations on the theme, "if you'd try just a little harder you'd do fine." Anticipating this attitude caused my anxiety to skyrocket at the mere thought of asking for accommodations, which made it well nigh impossible for me to follow through with the amount of persistence that scheduling and planning for a meeting on my own would have required. When I even thought about it, my vocal affect would drop and I'd be on the verge of a panic attack.*
>
> *Having an advocate to help me get through the panic and plan how to present my needs was invaluable – even so it was extremely difficult. (Sarah Knudsen, personal communication, January 19, 2004)*

Summary and Conclusion

In this chapter we looked at the IEP as an agent for developing skills in self-advocacy and disclosure. The process can be started with children from a young age by letting them know when they do something well and beginning with simple person-centered planning. By moving the student to the center of the IEP process, as opposed to serving as an optional source of information, the IEP team can get important information from the person who is most intimately aware of his or her own needs. The beauty of this method is that in addition to the IEP and procedures already in place, it teaches students self-advocacy and disclosure skills in a way similar to how other subjects are taught. Additionally, students can integrate their mathematics, reading, writing, and other skills as well in a real-world project in a meaningful way.

If Martin, described at the opening of this chapter, had been given the opportunity to develop his own IEP as an equal member of his educational team, college would undoubtedly have been less traumatic for him. He would have learned when, how, and to whom to go in order to disclose his placement on the autism spectrum within the context of self-advocacy. There is widespread agreement that math, reading, the arts and other subjects are vital for enabling students to pursue a fulfilling and productive life. Yet, skills in self-advocacy and disclosure are equally important since they allow those with special needs access to accommodations to achieve the same goals for their own well-being and to the benefit of all of society.

*Diagnosed with "atypical development with strong autistic tendencies," **Stephen Shore** was viewed as "too sick" to be treated on an outpatient basis and recommended for institutionalization. Nonverbal until the age of 4, with much help from his parents, teachers, and others, Stephen is now completing his doctoral degree in special education at Boston University with a focus on helping people on the autism spectrum develop their capacities to the fullest extent possible.*

In addition to working with children and talking about life on the autism spectrum, Stephen presents and consults nationally and internationally on adult issues pertinent to advocacy and disclosure, education, relationships, and employment, as discussed in his book, Beyond the Wall: Personal Experiences with Autism and Asperger Syndrome, *and numerous articles.*

He also serves on the board of the Autism Society of America, as board president of the Asperger's Association of New England, and is on the Board of Directors for Unlocking Autism, the Autism Services Association of Massachusetts, MAAP Services, and other autism spectrum-related organizations.

Stephen is executive director of Autism Spectrum Disorder Consulting and adjunct faculty at Salem State College and Emerson College.

References

American Psychiatric Association. (2000). *Diagnostic and statistical manual of mental disorders of the American Psychiatric Association* (4th ed., text revision). Washington, DC: Author.

Bandura, A. (1986). *Social foundations of thought and action: A social cognitive theory.* Englewood Cliffs, NJ: Prentice Hall.

Bandura, A. (1995). Exercise of personal and collective efficacy in changing societies. In A. Bandura (Ed.), *Self-efficacy in changing societies* (p. 2). Cambridge, UK: Cambridge University Press.

Bandura, A. (1997). *Self-efficacy, the exercise of control.* New York: W. H. Freeman and Company.

deCharms, R. (1972). Personal causation training in the schools. *Journal of Applied Social Psychology, 3,* 95-113.

deCharms, R. (1992). Personal causation and the origin concept. In C. P. Smith (Ed.), *Motivation and personality: Handbook of thematic content analysis* (pp. 325-333). Cambridge, UK: Cambridge University Press.

Field, S. (1996). Self-determination: Instructional strategies for youth with learning disabilities. *Journal of Learning Disabilities, 29*(1), 40-52.

Field, S., Martin, J., Miller, R., Ward, M., & Wehmeyer, M. (1998). *A practical guide for teaching self-determination.* Reston, VA: The Council for Exceptional Children.

Goffman, E. (1963). *Stigma: Notes on the management of spoiled identity.* New York: Simon and Schuster.

Grandin, T., & Duffy, K. (2004). *Developing talents: Careers for individuals with Asperger Syndrome and high-functioning autism.* Shawnee Mission, KS: Autism Asperger Publishing Company.

A guide to the individual education plan program. Office of Special Education Programs. Retrieved March 20, 2003, from http://www.ed.gov/offices/OSERS/OSEP/Products/IEP_Guide/.

Hughes, C., & Carter, E. W. (2000). *The transitions handbook: Strategies high school teachers use that work!* Baltimore: Paul H. Brookes Publishing Company.

Lefcourt, H. M. (1982). *Locus of control.* Mahwah, NJ: Lawrence Erlbaum Associates.

Lynch, R., & Gussel, L. (1996). Disclosure and self-advocacy regarding disability-related needs: Strategies to maximize integration in postsecondary education. *Journal of Counseling and Development, 74,* 352-356.

May, R. (1983). *The discovery of being: Writings in existential psychology.* New York: Norton.

McGahee, M., Mason, C., Wallace, T., & Jones, B. (2001). *Student-led IEPs. A guide for student involvement.* Arlington, VA: Council for Exceptional Children.

McGahee-Kovac, M. (2002). *A student's guide to the IEP* (2nd ed.). Washington, DC: National Information Center for Children and Youth with Disabilities. Retrieved March 23, 2002, from http://www.nichcy.org/pubs/stuguide/st1.htm.

National Information Center for Children and Youth with Disabilities. (2002). *Technical assistance guide: Helping students develop their IEPs.* Washington, DC: Author. Retrieved March 23, 2002, from http://www.nichcy.org/pubs/stuguide/ta2.htm.

Sawyer, B. (2000). One day in my life. In J. Goodman, D. Jekel, & P. Schwarz (Eds.), *Disclosure and Asperger's Syndrome: Our own stories* (p. 14). Newton, MA: Asperger's Association of New England.

Shore, S. (2003a). *Beyond the wall: Personal experiences with autism and Asperger Syndrome* (2nd ed.). Shawnee Mission, KS: Autism Asperger Publishing Company.

Shore, S. (2003b). Disclosure for people on the autism spectrum. In L. Willey (Ed.), *Asperger syndrome in adolescence: Living with the ups, the downs, and things in between* (p. 25). London: Jessica Kingsley Publishing.

Wehmeyer, M. L. (1996). Self-determination as an educational outcome: Why is it important to children, youth, and adults with disabilities? In D. J. Sands & M. L. Wehmeyer (Eds.), *Self-determination across the lifespan: Independence and choice for people with disabilities* (pp. 17-36). Baltimore: Paul H. Brookes Publishing Company.

CHAPTER 4

Being Your Own Case Manager

Roger N. Meyer

This chapter presents a distillation of the way I operate as a wrap-around case manager for others. Readers will gain some insights I have learned along the way of steering my own cases with providers, the most significant of which have been Vocational Rehabilitation and Social Security. From mistakes I made, and from lessons learned about some of the implacable problems with Vocational Rehabilitation, I have emerged as an independent paid advocate for others and a contractor to the very agency that turned down my request for technical assistance on my way to becoming a self-employed consultant. As an Aspie, "I did it my way."

When I was diagnosed with AS at the age of 55, I was approaching the end of my career as a cabinetmaker. My diagnosis and the understanding I gained from it led me further in the direction I have taken throughout my life as an advocate and educator, although I was never previously paid for that work. During my "previous life," I was a community mental health and organized labor activist, apprentice instructor and community mediator.

I never thought I would use the education I got with my B.A. in political science. I was wrong! I am a "systems person" and a policy wonk. I love learning about how systems and the people in them work. A year after my diagnosis, I founded the Portland Adult Asperger Syndrome Support Group and co-founded Oregon Parents United, a special education parent and student rights organization. Both are in their sixth year of operation. I became a peer counselor and disability advocate in a center for independent living. With a clinical social worker colleague and friend, I have participated for the past three years in a multidisciplinary clinical study group developing best practices in counseling AS adults and their family members.

In my new career, I have managed cases on behalf of individuals with AS, traumatic brain injury, organic brain disease, and profoundly disabling specific learning disabilities. In various capacities, I have represented clients in a large number of systems, including child welfare, adult protective services, Social Security, adult and juvenile community justice, special education, Vocational Rehabilitation, developmental disabilities services, disabled student services, unemployment insurance, adult medicine, and mental health services. I have also advocated on behalf of clients in postsecondary education and employment ADA appearances.

Recently, I stepped beyond disability interests into community politics as the elected president of my neighborhood association, a member of an urban renewal area political action committee, and president of my condominium association. For two years, I have been a Multnomah County Commissioner on the Housing and Community Development Commission and member of a county committee on special needs housing. In that role, I have combined a life-long interest in affordable housing and the comprehensive mix of public and private social services for those hardest to house.

As a mediator for 25 years, I have learned an invaluable lesson: *Conflict is a positive force. Successful resolution of differences can move people into self-discovery and empowerment.*

Why Should You Be Your Own Case Manager?

Many benefits and services are available to adults that can only be accessed through agencies and adult programs. Society expects adults to conduct as much of their business as they can. If you want to better manage your own affairs with agencies and providers, this chapter is for you. Throughout this chapter, the term "providers" refers to individual professionals as well as agencies and institutions. Here are some examples of providers and agencies:

- Student and adult special housing services and counselors
- Health care professionals (doctors and other specialists)
- Mental health services or psychological counselors
- Vocational Rehabilitation and specialized employment services
- Skills trainers and independent living advisors
- Disabled student center counselors, academic advisors and student career advisors
- Money managers and representative payees
- Peer counselors, disability rights advocates and attorneys
- Personal care attendant agencies and personal care attendants
- Social Security and other disability benefits public agencies

When you walk through a provider's door, you are already labeled as a *client, patient, consumer* or *case*. These terms imply that providers expect you to be passive, compliant, and uncritical. They are disempowering terms. Professional case managers, on the other hand, are persons with power. They operate in systems dominated by power relationships. What legitimates their power is their self-knowledge and knowledge about the system. To be a good case manager, you must be clear about your intentions. Others understand your intentions based on your words, your deeds and your public behavior.

What you say (your words) must be unambiguous. *What you do* (your deeds) must be consistent with what you say you will do and what a reasonable person would expect you to do. Your public behavior must be purposeful, polite and represent your best behavior.

This chapter will introduce you to the basic rules of conduct practiced by good case managers. Good case managers understand themselves. They know how to behave under conditions of stress and act appropriately when they are in conflict with others. Good case managers also understand agency rules and operating procedures. This chapter also describes conditions case managers operate under, and how they do their job under favorable *and* unfavorable conditions. Finally, the last part of the chapter covers basic concepts of negotiation. Since you have decided to be your own case manager, you must learn the basics of how to negotiate for what you need.

Asperger Syndrome and Rules

This section presents concepts governing your self-understanding about how you think and act in public. "Public" characterizes all of your conduct as manager of your own case. If you are not clear about your own standards about how you think and act – your personal rules – you will not understand providers' rules governing how they think and act. This section also discusses how change affects people's thoughts and actions.

Be Clear About Your <u>Own</u> Rules

Everyone has rules they live by. In general, folks with AS are more rule-oriented than others. We believe that there should be rules for everything. We also believe that when we understand those rules, this knowledge will help us understand the world. It is important to be clear about your rules as they affect your thoughts and behavior. Some of your own rules refer to your notions of right, wrong and fairness. Other personal rules refer to the way you think and do things.

It is not enough that you know what your rules are. Others must know about them as well. Others expect you to be explicit and clear-spoken about what you expect from them. Your expectations about others stem from your personal rule system.

To help you be clear about your own rules, consider making a three-part written list of your rules. The first part should contain your "core" values. These are the values you live by. For example, you are honest. Write down "honest." You are reliable. Write down "reliable." You mean what you say. So, write down "I mean what I say." Give providers a copy of this list, and tell them these are your basic values and that you expect them to respect your values. If a provider has a file for your case, ask the provider to place the list in your case file.

The second part of your written list should refer to things about you that providers should know about how you think and act in order to understand you better. Consider giving your providers this list, but do not expect the written list to "speak for itself." Review your list with providers and give them clear examples for each item on the list.

Here is what I mean. Let us say you write, "I become overwhelmed when people talk too fast. When I am overwhelmed, I become agitated. Sometimes I just shut down." Be sure to tell your provider what he or she can do to correct a situation that is starting to go bad. You know yourself best. You have an obligation to tell your provider that you are getting overwhelmed. Second, tell the provider what he or she can do to help.

Here is an example of this two-step process: "I'm starting to get overwhelmed. I can't keep up with what you're saying. Could you please slow down and repeat what you just said, maybe using different words?"

The third part of your written list should identify things that are important to you sometimes, but not all of the time. This is a list of your *tolerances*. Be very explicit. For example, you are a neat person and you prefer that other people be neat as well. However, you know some people are not neat. This means that while you would like a certain condition to be so, you have learned to live with the fact that it is not always going to happen with other people.

Here is an example and a challenge: You are having trouble writing a paper or a report. You need to talk with your instructor or your supervisor to get guidance. You know his or her office looks like a tornado hit it. Are you going to let this lack of neatness prevent you from getting the help you need?

It is very important that you become aware of your tolerance level. Write out your tolerance list but keep it to yourself! This list will change over time. It will change because each new positive life experience presents you with an opportunity to become more tolerant.

Know What Other People's Rules Are

Providers have *their* own rules. It is your responsibility to learn about their rules. Sometimes providers tell you about their rules. Often they do not. However, even if they do not tell you their rules, they still *act* according to them. You can discover their rules using other means, the most important of which are study and observation.

For example, it is safe to assume that persons who take better general care of themselves in terms of dress, personal hygiene, and so on, are better treated by providers. While this is not always the case, it is a good general rule, because the rule itself reflects how society in general treats people based upon their appearance. The provider is no different than "society." He or she has adopted an unwritten dress code for clients. In the waiting area, you notice some people who have very poor self-care and are sloppily dressed, with dirty or torn clothes. There may be other clients who "dress up" for their appointments. Guess who is likely to be taken more seriously by a provider? It is not unreasonable for you to conclude that dressing for success is better than looking as though you just came in from a one-week hike.

Understanding the Interplay Between Rules and Change

One diagnostic criterion for Asperger Syndrome is that AS individuals have trouble dealing with change. Things happen all the time that we cannot control. It may take us time to prepare for changes in others' routines. We generally like to be notified if things are going to be different. Some of us do not deal well in public when change happens. We may lose our temper, become irritable, stubborn, or shut down. As your own case manager and as a person with Asperger Syndrome, you must be acutely aware of how you respond publicly when others change their rules.

Some providers' rules change slowly. Others change more frequently. You *must* accept the fact that this is the way it is.

Rules That Change Slowly

Provider rules that dictate *how* things are done are called *procedural rules*. These rules generally change slowly. For the most part, procedural rules are written. In order to ensure uniform use, these rules are published in regulations, manuals, memoranda, orientation videos and public notices. Procedural rules often describe provider responsibilities and client rights and responsibilities. Some procedural rules are posted in waiting areas, and they may be printed in materials handed to you for your first appointment with a provider.

Rules That Change More Often

Other rules change more frequently. Rules that affect people's behavior are called *rules of practice*. They are often unwritten. Rules of practice are designed to keep relationships running smoothly, especially during or following a time of change. Providers are more likely to share these rules with you because everyone needs predictability in interpersonal relationships.

Budget cuts and agency reorganization often force providers to change their behavior towards one another and toward their clients. You can discover these rules of practice by observation or by asking people about them. For example, your agency caseworker may have his or her caseload doubled, or may cover for another caseworker out on leave or vacation. This change in practice may affect how often your provider can see you. As a result, your provider may ask you to send things in writing rather than call as often as you normally do. If you notice these changes, ask about them. However, it is unrealistic for you to ask that things go back to the way they were just because you are upset with the change in practice.

Facts about Rules of Any Kind

In his essay "Self Reliance," Ralph Waldo Emerson wrote, "A foolish consistency is the hobgoblin of little minds." This means that rigid adherence to rules – any rules – is not useful.

- Rules can be bent, broken, twisted, ignored, expire, or become irrelevant.
- Some rules are contradictory.
- Two or more systems with the same purpose may have contradictory rules.
- Stated or not, there are rules for good days and separate rules for bad days.
- *We break our own rules all the time.*
- The world out there is not always nice and fair.
- The system expects you to work with good players and bad players.

It would be ideal to live in a nice world where everything is fair. Unfortunately, the more you expect *nice* and *fair*, the more disappointed you will be. When you manage your own case, you must accept the fact that the world is as it is! Things are not always fair. Indeed, we must deal with people who break or alter rules.

We sometimes break our own rules. We make up new ones and discard and modify old rules that no longer meet our needs. Here is an example: You have told people you do not like to talk on the telephone. However, while managing your own case you have realized that important business is conducted on the telephone. Identify a counselor or friend who can help you get used to talking on the phone using role-plays and practice. Now, let us assume that your training has been successful. With the change in your personal behavior, you have changed or laid aside one of your rules: I do not like to talk on the phone. To other people who expect you to follow your old rule, you have broken or changed that rule.

Sometimes it is important to tell others you have changed your rules. Other times, people can tell from your new behavior that you have adopted a different rule. *If you believe that others should know of your rule change, do not wait for them to guess. Tell them.*

Case Managers Deal with Difficult People and Tough Situations All the Time

In every agency and profession, there are people who are easy to get along with and others who are not so easy to get along with. There are people who are nice and competent. There are also people who are *not* easy to get along with, but who are very competent at what they can do for you. There are people who are nice some of the time, but not so pleasant at other times. They, like you, have their moods. Because you have moods, you may be nice or less than nice on any given day. The fact of your moodiness is something your provider has to deal with.

For these reasons, when you walk into an agency or deal with providers, think first of the purpose that people working there serve and their "character" second. That is the way the folks who have hired them think of them. Hiring authorities do not expect their employees to be the same. That is because *everyone* has quirks. Unfortunately, some difficult people are inflicted on the consumer, the patient, "the case" – you.

When that happens, remember *your purpose in being there*. You are there to manage your case. You have to deal with these folks. However, sometimes you can side-step them. For example, you may be able to dress up a request to transfer your case to someone else using reasons other than the fact that the person supposedly helping you is a jerk.

An important subrule: Do not call real jerks "jerks." Everyone knows they are jerks. Professionals "stuff" their opinions about unpleasant people and bad situations all the time. If you want to succeed in handling your own case, this is one kind of personal opinion about others you must "stuff."

More Facts about Hidden Rules

We violate hidden rules all the time because we are not aware of them because they are rarely written down (hence the term "hidden"). Hidden rules govern how people "in the system" get along and work with each other. A hidden rule may be, *"In the event of disagreement, talk with your provider first. If your provider cannot help you, go to the next level of supervision. Do NOT go directly to the head of the agency to resolve a 'lower-level issue'!"* By skipping steps, you might get your problem resolved the first time, but because you jumped the chain of command, your provider may become wary of dealing with you in the future. That is, your provider now has reason to believe that rather than work through conflict with him/her, you will "go over his or her head."

AS individuals fear making mistakes that violate unwritten rules. Because we are not sure that there are such rules, or we do not know what they are, we can make mistakes. Global, generalized fear can make us indecisive. It also can cause some of us to be impulsive. We do things or say things "first" to avoid making a mistake later. Many times we guess wrong. We then become known as impulsive *and* as persons with poor judgment.

For case managers, indecision and impulsivity are negative traits. Faced with a case manager with these character traits, providers may begin to take back some responsibilities they have shared with you. They may conclude that they cannot sustain a good working relationship with you.

Even though these rules are almost never written down or otherwise stated, you can find out about them. To do that, you must (a) trust others, and believe what they tell or show you about these rules; and (b) trust yourself. People display self-trust by thinking and acting consistently. If you are of "a different mind" every time you consider taking an action, others are not responsible for your confusion. You are.

You are not the only person who appreciates consistency and predictability. Others do as well. Knowing that you have trouble figuring out hidden rules, you must determine whether an action you intend to take is consistent with action(s) you have taken in the past. If it is a different course of action, you might violate one or more hidden rules. Again, share your dilemma with a trusted friend or counselor who knows about hidden rules and who can help you identify them and obey them. Listen to that person's feedback. If he or she cannot figure out "where you are coming from," providers may have the same difficulty understanding you. Only, the provider might be too polite to tell you. If a provider starts acting differently than you expect, it may be because you have disregarded or broken a hidden rule.

Understanding Power Relationships

Some of the most important hidden rules in a system have to do with who has power over others and how that power is exercised. Power and the politics of power play an enormous role in your relationship with a provider. Power is sometimes obvious. "Politics" is not. Politics determines who has the real *power* and how actors in the system handle power. To manage your own case, you must know who has *real* power in the system. There are two steps to understanding political power, understanding yourself and understanding others.

Understanding Yourself

You must understand how you act and react to the whole "idea" of power. This is where many of us with AS get stuck. We have lofty notions about justice and fairness, and then plug our feelings about fair treatment and equality into a social context where relationships are often based upon the raw exertion of power. The result is that the harder we push our case based upon our notions of fairness, the harder the system may resist us. As a result, we end up with two campaigns on our hands: managing our case and fighting a "fairness war."

Some people can manage two such campaigns at once. Most of us with AS cannot. We do not multitask well. Faced with two concerns, we may become confused. We may mistake taking care of an unimportant detail (unimportant to the outcome of our case) first before tackling a major issue. When others observe our public displays of confusion, distractibility, or loss of focus, their respect for us as managers of our own case plummets. *Loss of respect equals loss of power.*

An important lesson to be learned here is to *keep your eyes on what you want* from a provider. Stay focused. Do not get distracted into a naked power struggle over "fairness" while seeking your prime objective.

Examine Your Thoughts and Feelings about Power

You must take personal responsibility for your feelings. Otherwise, you may act or react to power inappropriately. You could be consistent (and wrong) or inconsistent (and confusing) to others. Thinking incorrectly either way, your conduct may cause others to treat you as an untrustworthy "loose cannon" and cut off your access to persons of power.

Learn to Be "Appropriately" Consistent

Think of the idea of "foolish consistency" mentioned earlier. Being foolishly consistent means you may act from only a limited vocabulary of rules (thoughts) and behaviors. Very often, given a new context, your old rules and behaviors do not work. Connect with someone who can train you to expand how you perceive new situations and how you then act in those redefined situations. Seek out a coach, counselor, or advisor skilled in helping people expand their behavioral repertoire, which in turns expands their range of attitudes towards problem-solving. Counselors who practice effective cognitive behavioral therapy approaches modified for persons with Asperger Syndrome are best qualified to do this work with you.

Good counseling should produce word and behavior scripts for you that contribute to your *appearance of consistency* to others. Between the work sessions, practice with a safe person. Initially, your thoughts will not gel with your rehearsed behavior and verbal scripts. But as you practice, your comfort level with things that are not perfect in your mind will increase. Successfully acting the part takes a lot of energy, but acting like a professional involves just that: *acting*. Professionals succeed by gently bluffing and faking their way through difficult situations. You can too.

Dealing with Stress

Stress is built into power relationships. As persons with AS, we are very susceptible to stress. Stress can cause you to act and think inconsistently, revert to childlike behaviors and/or shut down. You may also become temperamental and aggressive. Further, you could mistakenly attribute your own mental state to others. For example: You may think and act aggressively towards others because you *think* they have the same feelings towards you. That may not be the case at all. *Assuming things without checking them out to see whether they are true or not is foolish and dangerous.*

You operate in inherently stressful settings when you deal with agencies and service providers. Therefore, it is important that you understand your unique responses to stress. Begin this process by working with a counselor or friend who can help you accurately monitor your stress level under safe "practice conditions." As you learn to manage low levels of stress, increase the level of stress in each practice session and work on controlling yourself under those conditions. With practice, you can desensitize yourself to certain known stressors. You can avoid some environmental stressors. And you can request certain reasonable accommodations that will reduce your stress to a manageable level. For example, if you know that extraneous office noise and conversation elevates your stress, ask to meet in a quiet room.

One way of desensitizing yourself is to work with a counselor or advisor to develop a written *stress-inducers* checklist that you can later consult to "check your feelings out at the door" before you visit a provider or make an important phone call. For example, if you have had a bad night of sleep before making an important visit or phone call, ask yourself what effect sleep deprivation has upon your ability to focus and accurately hear what others are saying and doing. If you know that you are likely to act or think quite differently "today" but still want to keep the appointment, share what sleep deprivation is likely to do to your ability to handle yourself professionally with your provider in advance of starting your work with that provider. Even if you behave differently today, your provider is likely to understand why, provided you have informed him/her in advance. As an added benefit, you will not find yourself demanding so much of yourself because you know you behave differently when you are sleep-deprived.

Another way of dealing with stress and keeping your power is to study how your provider responds to stress. In this case, "the provider" may be an individual person and/or the whole system you are dealing with. Such knowledge allows you to "keep your cool" to use your power wisely and get your job done. As an example, you know that sleep deprivation is a stressor. Ask how your provider deals with sleep deprivation, noisy working conditions, or lots of distractions. You may be quite surprised at what you hear. An added benefit to "studying" your provider this way is that you've employed a personal research tool in a very genuine, empathetic way.

Understanding How Others Deal with Power

In addition to understanding yourself, you must also know how others in the system understand power relationships and how they use that knowledge responsibly. Persons with AS have substantial boundary issues. That means that we sometimes unknowingly bumble and crash through people's privacy barriers. We can be tactless and insensitive when dealing with persons at different levels of authority and power.

Ask someone you trust how he or she relates to someone in a position of power. First, accurately set the scene for him or her. Then, ask the person to be direct and tell you or show you how he or she would handle a given interaction. Remember: We have a hard time with "subtle." Advisors may be uncomfortable with being direct or blunt with you. They may view being direct as being impolite and disrespectful. So, in order for them to teach you, you must give them permission to be direct and blunt so that you can learn from them.

The Pyramid of Escalation

When dealing with outsiders, providers work on a "sliding scale" of formality. Unless they come under attack, their initial approach is to act within the rules, but once they get to know you, they may act more informally. While there are rules, people do not make a big deal about them. Successful case management often takes place at this level. However, if you come across to your provider in a cantankerous, inconsistent or rigid way, the provider may decide that dealing formally with you is safer. That is, because of your behavior, people may act defensively. The more this happens, the drier the gears get that once were greased for meshing smoothly. Your whole relationship can grind to a halt. This is definitely where you do not want to be. Remember: when repairing a deteriorating condition, losing your temper is not a good choice. Neither is stomping away.

There is one correct way to handle this kind of escalation. It involves two steps. First, *make sure you are not the problem causing it*. The best way to find out is to ask. Do it with sensitivity, but do it. Depending on the answer, you may need to take a break and excuse yourself to do some personal work to polish up your act. If you need to do that, tell your provider that is what you will do. Then do it.

Second, find out how you can *assist in de-escalating the situation* and ramping the level of tension downwards. Again, do not guess, ask. Given the answer(s), go through those de-escalation steps. For example, if your provider tells you that you were calling impulsively or at bad times of the day, promise to save up your issues by writing them down and compiling a list and agree to call less often. Agree to pay attention to the length of your call by practicing using a timer or a watch, or ask the provider how much time he or she has to talk with you and abide by that limit. Offer to call or leave messages only at times that are convenient to the provider. As you get more in control of your problem behavior, you earn good will and the reputation of being a good problem-solver.

Provider Rules about Provider Social Relationships with Outsiders

These are the most difficult rules to discover for people who are not a part of the system, whether they are on the autism spectrum or not. As we saw above, rules involved in the pyramid of escalation become noticeable when things start to break down. But the rules we are talking about here are different. They are informal and are likely to *remain* hidden. These rules refer to a kind of "underground economy" or, to put it another way, a hidden but powerful means of exchange between systems.

Consider Yourself a System of One

Social exchange is built on a three-legged foundation, much like a milking stool. Here are the legs:

- power
- trust
- good will

Take away any one of the legs from that stool and you are sure to fall over.

Power is "a given feature." Authority and capacity to do things is legislated or conferred by society. But trust and good will, the other two legs of the metaphorical stool, are not "givens." You cannot buy them. They must be earned. In order for the exchange system to work smoothly, these two elements must be more or less equal between participants.

Keep this idea in mind when considering what you deserve from any provider. Ask yourself whether you extend trust and good will to the provider at about the same level he or she has extended these qualities to you. If you have not, you have some personal work to do.

Here is an example of personal work on the "trust issue." You have had a terrible time trusting other service providers. Using the milking stool metaphor, trust for you is a weak leg. With a personal counselor, friend or coach, list specific reasons identifying who, what, when, and why you have trouble trusting a provider. ("I don't like her/him" is *not* a good answer.)

With that same person, determine what is objectively different about this provider or this agency. Allow your counselor, coach or friend to grill you about those differences. Give honest answers. Let them also work with you about your all-or-nothing thinking and your black-and-white judgment about people. If it turns out that you cannot see the difference between old and new, yesterday and today, that situation and this situation, this person and that person, you are not ready to manage your own case.

It is as simple as that. You need more personal work. If you charge ahead, insisting that you can manage your case anyway, you are headed for disappointment and may ruin your chances for future attempts with the same provider.

Individual people in a system represent their agencies and their professions. Their relationships embody the subcultural history of connections forged between their systems. As individuals, they have complex connections with one another. As an outsider, you have very tenuous connections with the system at this level of complexity.

Most individuals with AS have "boundary problems." Many of us are unaware of how rude or disrespectful our conduct is if we impose ourselves on others. Think of your relationship to a provider in the system as similar to being a stranger visiting a public park. If an organized team was playing soccer or a family was holding a picnic, could you just go over to them and demand to join the game or the picnic? No.

You only have a right to be in the park, not to demand membership in already formed groups and ongoing activities. If you were to make such a demand, your conduct would be considered rude, maybe even outrageous.

As your own case manager in someone else's "system," your status is that of guest, not member. Your right to be treated as anything more than a guest is totally dependent upon how you conduct yourself.

Two Notes of Caution

1. *Many adults with AS have unrealistic, untested notions of their social acceptance by others.*
   If you hang around for a while, you can learn some of the oral history and unwritten rules of the system. But remember that regardless of how familiar you think you can be with others in the system, you will always be viewed as an outsider. That is not bad. It is just how things are.

2. *Be aware of dual or multiple relationships.*
   Your primary relationship with the provider is as manager of your own case. You engage in high-risk behavior if you think you can also develop a friendship, intimate relationship, or business (financial or seller/buyer) relationship with that same person at the same time. All of these arrangements are considered multiple relationships, and all such relationships impose complications upon your primary relationship with a provider.

   Many agencies and professions have ethical rules or "standards of practice" regulations that prohibit dual or multiple relationships with clients. Those rules are in place to protect persons who are clients, patients, or consumers of agency services. The real problem with dual or multiple relationships is that, in most instances, you are a person of unequal power compared to your provider.

Pursuing such relationships is not considered good professional conduct. Minimally, such relationships can endanger the provider's primary relationship with you.

Rules about Relationships with Providers

Folks with AS have trouble with relationships. When you manage your own case, here are some basic rules about relationships.

- *The Best Behavior Rule*
  Be sure to observe this rule. For example, you cannot afford to make many "mood mistakes." If you are unsure about your mood, follow this two-part subrule: (a) if in doubt, check yourself out with others; and (b) if they say that your mood is not good, do not argue. What is the point? Accept their observation: you are not ready to deal with providers right now.

- *The Life Raft Rule of Survival*
  Do not make waves, and do not do or say things that threaten others. Visualize a shipwreck on the high seas. You are a passenger, the ship has gone down and you have found a life raft and clambered aboard to join the other survivors. For whatever reason, you start to get upset. You thrash about, knocking people around. You slash at the soft rubber of the life raft and damage it.

  Fearing for their safety, folks decide to tie a rope around you and throw you overboard on a tether until you have cooled down. You are not drowning, but you are not out of danger. They tell you to think about why you are in the water. While they repair the raft, they expect you to come up with answers *they* can live with before they pull you aboard again. You must offer a genuine apology plus a believable assurance to be better behaved in the future.

  Moral of the story: What you think is only half of the solution to any problem. *Others make their determinations about you all the time.* They take into consideration the same things that concern you: your predictability and your willingness to problem-solve, assume responsibilities and behave professionally.

- *Nobody Likes a Sourpuss Rule*
  Even sourpusses do not like themselves. When you start feeling and
  acting like a sourpuss, you cannot afford to "go with the flow."
  Others are not in control of your moods. You are. When things start
  going downhill, seek out someone who can help you understand
  your moods. Professionals seek supervision regularly to "stay on an
  even keel." So should you. Regular work of this kind is called professional development.

  You may have some repair work to do on a damaged relationship
  before you resume your business. Calm down and use the right
  mental tools to (a) recognize that repair is needed; and (b) choose
  among the best means for managing your emotions.

- *The Rule of First Impressions*
  Humans relate to one another largely based upon first impressions.
  Individuals with AS have trouble giving up first impressions even if
  later facts do not support holding onto them. For example, if you
  get bad feelings during a first encounter, you might later avoid a
  provider based on those feelings. It is not important to know why
  you ruminate, but you must accept that you do it. You have had an
  initial bad experience. So what? You are not the only one who oper-
  ates on the basis of first impressions. Nonautistic folks do so all the
  time. However, they correct those first impressions by determining
  whether later developments justify holding onto them. So can you.

  To get out of this rut, ask yourself, "Is my first impression always
  right?" Then ask, "Do I have good tools to check out whether my first
  impression is correct?" If you know that your initial take on a new situation is not always correct, you have earlier learned how to tune up
  your thoughts when things change following a first impression. Put
  those lessons to use now.

- *Being Aware of Taking Things Literally Rule*
  Folks with AS tend to take things literally. Accept this fact. Do you
  have accurate means of checking out other people's meaning of
  words, phrases, or actions? If others have told you that you do not,
  take their statements as the truth. Do not argue. Tell people that you
  take things literally. As long as you know that you often misinterpret

what people say, be proactive when you first meet them. For example, you could say, "I have a tendency to take what people say literally. I also miss things if the conversation is rushing along faster than I can follow it. Would you mind if I stopped the conversation to check my understanding of what you've just said?"

Note what is going on here. Without being asked to do so, most folks do not slow their conversation down on their own. In fact, if someone is convinced that you do not understand them, their "normal" response is to speed up what they say, repeating the same words in a higher-pitched voice. You need to stop this dynamic. By explaining yourself and asking them to slow down, you give nonautistic persons permission to slow down and let you process what they are saying. You may find your later conversations easier to handle. They may stop and "check in with you" to determine whether the pace of conversation is OK and whether the meaning of their words is the same as yours. Once you have started, do not leave this job to them. When things begin to get overwhelming, respectfully repeat your request of them to slow down. Then check out the meaning of confusing words, phrases, or concepts.

What we have been discussing above is improving your communication skills. There are two other useful things to think about:

- Becoming a better active listener makes for more effective communication.

- Mistakes are often better teachers than successes.

Learn to Listen Carefully, Accurately, and Actively

Active listening consists, principally, of giving another person a chance to talk while you indicate, through a variety of techniques, that you have heard and understood what they mean. Active listening is a teachable skill. Many nonautistic individuals need work on this skill because their active listening skills are quite poor. Reading about active listening does not teach people how to do it. The only way you learn to listen actively is to practice doing it with other people in a safe environment. There are classes at community colleges and community mediation programs that teach active listening skills. The cost is low, and the benefits are high.

Learn From Your Mistakes

Adults with AS are terrorized about making mistakes. Our fear tends to make us indecisive or impulsive. Often by the time we speak or act, things have passed us by, and we find ourselves in a perpetual game of catch-up. The worst part of this dynamic is that others may end up making decisions for us or about us that we should be making ourselves.

A good example of "too little too late" is what happens when you procrastinate over taking advantage of a one-time offer. Let us say you learn about a free skills training workshop or conference. Your provider is willing to sponsor your attendance. You do not respond to the offer. Unless you come up with a good excuse for not acting on this opportunity, the next time such an event comes up, your provider may not even mention it to you. Furthermore, the provider's expectation that you can take care of your own business has been lowered. If you miss too many of these opportunities, your provider may perceive your inaction as a sign of disinterest and therefore be less motivated to work with you.

The Mouse in the Maze – Learning from Mistakes

Think of a mouse in a maze smelling food somewhere at the end of the maze. The mouse is drawn to the smell. The hungry mouse wanders down many "false paths" and eventually arrives at the food. If you put the mouse back into the same maze with the same conditions, the mouse runs the maze a little faster. The mouse is learning. Without changing any conditions, if you repeat this exercise enough times, you will have a very smart mouse.

There are several lessons to be learned from this simple scenario.

- *Lesson one: the barriers are still there.* The maze has not changed.

- *Lesson two: the mouse does not sit in front of a barrier and ruminate about its miserable fate in not finding the food reward.*

- *Lesson three: the risk of running the maze is small and acceptable.*

In making each mistake when it first started out, the mouse did not fall through a trap door or get shocked on an electric grid or step onto a mousetrap. It just experienced a barrier. If you could get inside that mouse's brain at that time, you would hear something like, "Huh. That didn't work. I wonder if . . ." and then it is off and running in a different direction and making choices every time a barrier is encountered until finally, Voila, there is the reward. In other words, if you are at least as smart as the mouse, learn some lessons from how it learns from its mistakes.

This metaphor has other uses. Note that the mouse is not in competition with anyone. The mouse does not think about the consequences of not beating its own time during the next run. The mouse is a singular actor. You are a singular actor. Keep this in mind as you manage your case. Categorical comparisons with others are not appropriate.

Just a small addition to this general rule about not comparing yourself to others. If you do compare yourself *to* yourself, go easy. Remember: you have good days and bad days just like everyone else.

Navigating a confusing service system is very much like running a maze. The mouse learns – so can you.

Case Management Relationships Are Instrumental Relationships

I am going to say something that is very Aspie here, but it fits! Case management relationships are *political, instrumental relationships*. As your own case's manager, you enter into relationships with providers "up front" about wanting something from them. There is no beating around the bush, and no game playing about how and why case managers go about their business. Case management relationships are not as emotionally confusing as friendships and intimate relationships. The nature of professional practice, the way that all bureaucracies act, and the time-limited and functional limitations of an agency's mission or program distinguish an instrumental relationship from casual or intimate relationships with other people who are not providers.

Case managers rely on *power, information and knowledge* to do business. Those three elements are not primary factors in friendship or intimate relationships, both of which have entirely different rules of engagement. The following discussion focuses on the relationship between power, information and knowledge.

Knowledge Is Power

Understanding yourself, your own rules, and the system and its rules can lead to responsibly exercised power. In case management, all parties involved should be able to talk candidly and respectfully about power, inequality, and satisfactory outcomes. Although there are differences between your power and the power of those you deal with, you can determine just what can and cannot be done in your case by knowing the rules. Knowing the rules gets you halfway to success. Knowing how to handle yourself gets you through the other half. Successful outcomes result from well-managed relationships.

Bad Relationships Do Nothing to Advance Your Case

Abuse, underhanded dealings, manipulation, and fear due to unequal power and irresolvable control issues between the parties characterize bad relationships. Where you encounter *systemic* dysfunction and bad practice – meaning almost everyone in a system acts this way – consider finding a professional advocate or an attorney to help you. That is, if you need what a corrupt or bad system has to offer and there is no other way to get it, hand over the job of getting it to a "pro."

Deal with Your Bad Feelings about Good People

Do you get jealous of others who have had success with the system? Do you sometimes get angry with good people who try to help you? Do you worry about blowing folks away and/or depending on them too much? You can have these feelings. Everyone does. However, as a case manager you cannot afford to wallow in them.

If you keep coming on too strong, you have not learned from your mistakes. If you avoid doing things that could benefit you, you choose to avoid and you will be the loser. When – not if – you examine the reasons why you feel so aggressive or so immobilized, you can learn how you respond to challenges. The choice is yours to look at the effect of your emotions on your actions. When you "constantly run up against yourself" around making decisions, you are most likely caught in a whirlpool of dysfunctional thoughts and dysfunctional behaviors. Earlier, I recommended seeking out a counselor experienced in cognitive behavioral therapy. It works, but you have to be the one who recognizes your need to do some personal work to get beyond behaviors and thoughts that sabotage attaining your objectives, your case management goals.

Do You Have Problems Asking for Information?

Adults must make decisions. To make good decisions, you must be well informed. While some information is easy to access, other information is not. Most individuals with AS have trouble asking for help. This problem contributes to inefficient problem-solving. If you are to be your own case manager, you must be an efficient resource user. Hard-to-get information often involves laying bare the inner workings of a system or a program. That is precisely the kind of information case managers must have to get their clients what they need. For example, you may need to know how long it takes a provider to grant approval for a certain kind of request for benefits or services. You may not be able to get this information *directly*, but there are other ways of getting it. You can find out from other people.

Different Kinds of Asking

Even if you fully manage your own case, there may be some things you are not allowed to ask or do because of system rules. That is because others are responsible for these things. For example, you cannot issue your own checks for benefits. Other people do that. But you can still be sufficiently involved in managing your case to make sure that these other people follow their own rules. For example, if you know these rules, you can remind others about them without stepping out of line and appearing to be demanding. You may need practice knowing how to do that. Ask a friend or a counselor to role-play with you so that you find words and phrases that are contextually appropriate to your role at this stage of your case's progress.

You can ask to be included in certain decision-making processes. Doing so involves informed consent. One way of ensuring that you know the most about something you are asked to agree with is to seek advice or information from others.

When you manage your own case, there are things you are expected to do on your own. However, asking others to help may be the most efficient way to get what you need. For example, if you know someone who can explain a complicated procedure that they deal with all the time, ask them to summarize it for you. That may give you enough information to be sufficiently informed to understand a similar or identical procedure used by your provider.

Assessing the Risk of Asking for Help

Even for nonautistic people, asking for help can be risky. One risk is that you might appear stupid or inept. If you ask "the wrong way," that could happen. Another risk is that your timing, what you ask for, who you ask, how you ask, and even why you ask, may not be good given certain conditions.

Remember taking long trips when you were a child? Remember how irritated your parents got when you continually asked or worried about how far you had gone or how many miles away you were from your destination? You were a child then, and maybe your family were patient with you. But now you are an adult. Thinking and acting like a child does not work for adults. If you act in a childlike manner, you will be treated like a naughty child. For things known to take a long time, you must show patience. If you cannot manage your impulse to ask questions, find someone safe to work with you to modify your behavior. With such a trainer or coach, you can learn how to ask appropriate questions in a polite and adult manner.

How to Ask Questions and What Questions to Ask First

When you need information, think of yourself as an investigative reporter. Reporters use the "five w's and one h" questions: *who, what, when, where, why* and *how*. Rehearsal and practice in asking these reporters' questions will lead you to better choices, decisions and outcomes.

Who, what, when and *where* questions are easier to ask first. That is because they are *fact* questions. What you find out will help you determine your priorities in asking for additional information. Knowing that additional information will help you negotiate your way to getting what you need from your provider. For example, it is a lot easier to ask *who* has the information you need, and then ask them for it than asking that person *how* he or she came by that information. That is, asking people about *how* they do their job may be irrelevant unless you have to learn how to do their job. They could view your *how* questions as a threat. *How* questions could be experienced as rude and invasive. *How* may be none of your business.

Why and *how* questions are also tougher because they may be opinion questions. You may have strong personal opinions or strong ideas about "how to do things." Arguing over opinion issues when you first need facts is not going to help you. When more trust is established, you can ask opinion questions, but you must ask respectfully and be fully ready to listen and not argue.

It is OK to ask others to help determine what to do first, but you are ultimately responsible for what you do. Here are some tips about using helpers.

• *Spread Your Requests for Help Around Among Several People*
This prevents two mistakes. First, if you rely on one person, he or she may become disaffected by your always returning just to them. If you start with one person, do so with the idea of widening your circle of helpers. Ask whom else to ask when the person is busy, or who might have information that he or she does not have.

The second reason why you should not concentrate on just one person connects directly to the fear of making mistakes and how easily you may cast blame on others. Asking only one person allows you to indulge yourself by blaming somebody else for your own mistakes in judgment. This type of self-indulgence is not helpful. Professionals do not learn by blaming others.

It is OK to make mistakes when you ask for help. Everyone does. "Fine," you say. "I'm not everyone else. *I'm me.*" To which I answer, "OK, now where does that attitude get you?" It gets you exactly nowhere! You have just made an "I statement" with no other purpose than making an "I statement." It also means that you will not receive help by acting like a child in the throes of the terrible twos who walks around affirming only himself and being obnoxious. But you are not a two-year-old. You are an adult.

• *Mi Mi Mi Mi Mi!*
The only relatively successful adults I know of who have huge reputations for being self-centered are opera singers who warm up with their "mi mi mi mi mi's." Please note, though, that they are not singing "me me me me me!" And even with all of those "mi's," we know what they are doing. They are not making statements excluding everyone in the world except themselves. They are warming up their voices, their instruments, for a good performance.

If opera singers known for their huge egos warm up, what is to prevent us from doing that? Absolutely nothing. The only way we are going to get what we need is to *practice, practice, practice.*

Incidentally, throughout their successful careers, many accomplished opera singers visit their voice coaches regularly. Just because they are at the top of their form does not mean they do not seek feedback, training and advice. They do this to avoid damaging their voices and to improve their technique. You can use the help and advice of others to do the same thing.

- *Deal Responsibly with Stage Fright*
  Before they step on stage, experienced performers use their concern about "flubbing it" to their advantage. They do not let it overwhelm them. Instead, they use the "edge of excitement" to excel on stage. You can too, but you have to learn how to manage your performance anxiety. If you are terrorized by your fear of making mistakes, you have just identified a first priority for self-work before resuming the management of your case. *Practice making mistakes and then recovering from them* with a safe person like a trusted family member, friend, a counselor or an adult acting coach. Come up with scripts in your head as well as behaviors and words that you can use with strangers.

  Hint: Do not wait to act until you are "completely ready." Ready for what? The unexpected? No one is ever completely ready for that! The adult world is inherently risky. You learn to handle yourself by taking manageable risks, making mistakes, and then recovering from them and forging ahead. Adults learn more from their mistakes than from their successes.

AS and the Rocky Road to Negotiation

Negotiating is about learning how to make deals. Your provider has something you want: either a one-time benefit or a continuing benefit or service. You have something the provider wants: your fees may support the provider. That is, your showing up means the provider has a customer or client, and your status as customer or client is something the provider needs to stay in business.

Let us assume that by now you know about your rule system. You have learned about rules, generally, and your provider's rule system in particular. You have also learned to be efficient by asking for help when you need it, knowing that getting help from others will save you time.

Before you start to negotiate, let us look at two features of Asperger Syndrome that are likely to trip you up.

1. *Meet Your "Honest to a Fault" Demon*
   You may be disarmingly honest. That very feature of your AS can be a "plus" when it comes to managing your case. That is, because of your honesty, others trust you to be true to your word and mean what you say. Despite the positive side, however, one huge note of caution is warranted: *Sometimes your brand of honesty is not the best policy, or at least it is not the best policy for a given time or at given point in negotiations.* You may blurt things out that you cannot take back. You may be "right" but wrong in "telling." Your forthrightness might prompt you to tell all, to leave nothing in reserve. Never do this when you negotiate. It is unprofessional.

   Without being dishonest, professionals know how to hold things back, to keep issues or facts in reserve until the time is right to come out with them. Similarly, in chess, players do not reveal their next moves to opponents. In most card games, players do not let other players know what is in their hand until the right moment. Smart negotiation involves understanding these kinds of "rules of withholding." Let us say that your provider is Vocational Rehabilitation. You want to see how well you work with your counselor before you "spill all the beans" by talking about needs that VR cannot possibly satisfy but could help you get from another agency. If the relationship with your first counselor turns out to be a bad one, you do not want to appear to be a totally unreasonable or uncooperative client for the next coun-selor, who might be a better match for you.

2. *Check Your Words, Meanings and Assumptions*
   Do not assume that others understand what you mean. Test your assumptions by asking others to come up with their own words to describe what they think you are saying. At the same time, it is also fair for them to ask you to tell them in your own words what they just said. If either one of you is way off the mark, it is your mutual responsibility to get the picture clear before proceeding. Otherwise, each of you will babble on "past" the other person without being understood. Good active listening skills exercised by everyone ensure that this will not happen.

   Providers have their own jargon. As an outsider, you do not have to adopt their vocabulary completely, but you should understand it. The easiest way to learn their language is to ask them to "civilianize" or translate their terms to words whose meanings you both agree to. If your negotiations will be brief, ask them to use non-jargon language. If you expect your dealings to take longer, consider using some of their terms that you fully understand. It is courteous to do so. A good example is a common term used in the United States by state Vocational Rehabilitation services: Individualized Plan of Employment or IPE. Once you understand the term, consider using IPE as shorthand. Doing this is a courtesy and also indicates to the counselor that you understand what an IPE is.

Prevent Power Tripping Through Clear Communication

Unexplained, your words or behavior may confuse others. Sometimes they will tell you that; at other times they will not. That is when power tripping could start. Because your provider does not understand your behavior, you might find yourself being talked at rather than conversing in a reciprocal manner. By the time this happens, you may have no easy way to stop your provider from assuming things about you that are untested and untrue. Do not let this happen. Test others' assumptions by using the check-in and active listening techniques referred to above.

Do Not Play "Mind Games"

You must come to grips with reality by checking out your assumptions and determining other people's true intent, because, as a person with Asperger Syndrome, you cannot read others' minds very well.

With electronic and role-playing games, you can safely immerse yourself in the world of fantasy – you can lose the game without being hurt. But that does not hold true when managing your case. As a case manager, you are playing for real stakes. If you lose, it is often hard to get back what you have lost.

Be clear about your needs by testing your assumptions and accurately determining others' intentions. Do not play "bad-faith games." It is not other people's job to guess what is in your mind. It is your job to tell them. Do not turn your first meetings into a power struggle and a bout of playing hide-and-seek with words. When people ask you to explain what you mean, *do it.* When you do not understand what they mean, *tell them* you do not understand. Ask them to explain themselves right from the point when you start to get lost, not after you have been in a fog for some time. *When you share the meaning of your words, you are not "giving them away," nor are you giving your power away. You are sharing and relating.*

Many young children on the autistic spectrum fear sharing their thoughts with others. We are not children. However, when we are under stress, we can become very childlike in a distressing way. Hide-and-seek is a game that kids play for fun. Hide-and-seek for adults is not fun. You may get a childlike thrill from frustrating others – from "beating" them – but after a while, people will not take you seriously. Stay on that path and you lose your case. It is as simple as that.

Rules of Negotiation – Phase I

Negotiation involves understanding what you have to gain as well as what you might lose if you do not handle yourself in a professional manner. Here are some basic rules about negotiation.

Know Your Bottom Line

Your bottom line is what you *need*. Needs are different from *wants*. Needs are essential, whereas wants are things that are nice to have, but not essential. Knowing the difference between needs and wants tells others you have done a good job clarifying your priorities.

Before you start, make sure your needs can be satisfied by the provider you negotiate with. For example, if you need housing and the system cannot provide housing, housing should *not* be at the center of your discussion. However, there is an important exception to this rule. If what you can get from one source improves your chance of getting another need satisfied from another source, let the first provider know that.

Doing this can be risky, so run your idea by a knowledgeable person first. Ask the person how it sounds. Listen to what he or she says. Checking out your idea with someone else reduces the likelihood that you might squander your relationship with a provider by asking for something that the provider really cannot give you.

Know Their Bottom Line

Even if the person or the system says "no" to your bottom line, note *when* they first refuse. Keep your cool and ask yourself whether this will *always* be their response. It may be a response they always make as a part of their opening style or initial posture.

Also, there is a difference between *can't* and *won't*. *Can/can't* is often a matter determined by provider rules. *Will/won't* is often a function of your provider's personal temperament and individual judgment. If you have done your homework and you recognize your provider *can't* deliver all of what you ask for, that knowledge should guide your relationship with your first provider and with other providers who could contribute the missing pieces.

For example, let us say you want to become self-employed. In the United States, VR uses the concept of *comparable services and benefits* to determine what assets you have and what other benefits programs could contribute towards meeting the costs of your IPE. Understanding this concept, you should realize that Vocational Rehabilitation is not a venture capital bank. VR *can't entirely* capitalize your business venture. However, VR *can* support your plan by contributing *some* government assets, provided the financial marketing survey and management portions of your business plan are sound.

Here is an example of *will/won't:* If, according to business plan experts, your business plan *is* sound *and* the VR counselor is wrong or unreasonable in his/her judgment about its soundness, you could appeal your counselor's opinion and possibly win your case. If you win, it might be wise to consider changing counselors or even VR branch offices, because although you may have "won," you most likely will not remain on good terms with the person who said "no" and then was shown to be wrong upon appeal.

Be Aware of Time Management and Efficiency of Effort

Providers have certain work routines and habits. If you work your case well, you can save the providers time by doing some things they would otherwise do. Carefully point out the increasing number of tasks you are taking on.

Using the example of self-employment above, let us say you conduct a comprehensive and professional market survey of the field or business you are interested in. Your survey demonstrates that your planned venture is feasible, the employment market is growing in that field, and you could make a good living by being self-employed. Such surveys can be conducted by VR, but are often "done on the cheap." If you take the time to conduct one yourself, you are likely to be more thorough, and your results are likely to be more convincing. Working together with your provider, you may be able to move your case along faster. Your work contributes to the provider's *relative efficiency*, making the provider look good in the eyes of management. You are building a "good-will account."

In the future, you may be able to draw on it, but *do not* enter the relationship assuming that you can do so. That is because many things happen to providers that are not under your control. For example, the individual provider may leave or be transferred, or the program may shut down. In either instance, you have not really lost. You have gained in the sense that some of your good work has been put forward as self-less, done to help someone else without expectation of reward or recognition. That is a pretty good accomplishment for a person with AS.

Be Patient

Sometimes you may be ready to move ahead when your provider is not. Using the self-employment example, let us say that you need letters or official communication from your VR counselor to others right away. The problem is that this is quarterly report time at the agency, so the demands of the office do not allow your provider to jump at your command. What can you do? Take a break until the provider is ready. Set a date and time to meet in the future. Work on other aspects of your case that do not require your provider's time or attention. Stay busy with real work. Doing so keeps you from fixating on the future date and using that date as an excuse not to do anything else right now.

Earlier in this chapter we talked about power and power relationships. Negotiation involves the blending of interests – yours and theirs – and working with power differences. Successful negotiation involves a process where both parties recognize one another's point of view, know one another's interests and needs, and problem-solve a way to a mutually satisfactory resolution of their differences.

Negotiation – Phase II: Haggling, Part One

Good negotiators are good bargain-hunters. Even though "the system" seems to have all the power and you have very little, the system itself may offer good deals and bad deals.

Engage in Comparison Shopping

If you comparison-shop and "buy smart" in your everyday life, you already understand the concept of *intrinsic value*. As you shop, you may discover someone's bottom line is not really that solid – there is some "give." You may be able to go somewhere else and get what you need at a cheaper price. If he or she does not bargain seriously, you can tell the person with a higher price that you intend to do just that. Be careful how you do this, though, because upon further investigation, what may seem like bargains elsewhere may not be true bargains.

- *Agency and System Delusion: "We're the Only Place in Town"*
  Some providers think they are the only game going. But that may not be true. In dealing with providers, business and politics are very much intertwined. *Business* is involved in the sense that if shoppers do not think something is a good deal, they will stay away or leave. A business without customers has a hard time justifying keeping its doors open. *Politics* comes into play when people who pay the bills (taxpayers) assess provider performance by looking at meaningful outcomes, not just numbers and statistics. If service is poor or no service is being rendered at all and people are just going through the motions, bill-payers can pull the plug on the provider.

- *Your Negotiating Leverage – The Fact That You Are There*
  Your provider "needs" you as a customer as much as you need the provider – perhaps more. The last thing taxpayers want to hear is that customers leave or stay away because they can get what they need elsewhere and that their avoidance is a principled rejection of a bad deal or no deal at all.

  However, it is important for you to understand that some bureaucracies have incredible staying power despite failing to deliver the goods. Over time, some become sacred cows. Do not think that just because an agency is not effective it will go away and stop wasting tax money. Realizing that truth is part of politics too.

Take Advantage of Pilot Projects

If you hear of a pilot project that is a good match for you, do everything you can to access it. It may not be around for long. Your power, in this case, is that you *know* about this alternative. Confronted with your knowledge, providers who have said "no" up to now may support your interest in taking part in a program they have not heard of or thought of. When they do support your participation, make a special effort to thank them. Even though they were "just doing their job," your acknowledgment of their support may open more doors for you later on.

Do Not Show Attitude

We all have moods. If you are not good at monitoring your moods, ask others you trust to give you honest feedback. If they say you are in a bad mood, believe them. Most of us with AS are not good at putting on a smiley face if we feel lousy. Fight the temptation to impose yourself on others when you feel that way. This is known as "showing your attitude." It is unprofessional conduct.

Know When to Stop and Acknowledge Progress

A good negotiator knows when to stop pressing ahead and confirm progress already made. Acknowledging progress makes everyone feel good. Make a deliberate effort to thank providers for things they have done. Even though this may be "their job," acknowledging their support with a genuine show of gratitude by recognizing specific things they have done will build good will.

Negotiation – Phase II, Haggling, Part Two – Wrapping Things Up

Before concluding your relationship with a provider, take time to review what has worked and what has not worked so well. Professional case managers do this all the time. They review their work privately and with others. They solicit feedback from others about how well they are doing. They do this because they know that good results do not just happen by accident.

Here are questions good case managers ask themselves.

Do I Understand and Respect My Limits?

You may have unrealistic expectations, either high or low, about what you can accomplish. Make sure that what you are striving for is worth expending the energy necessary to achieve it. The more important something is to you, the more important it is for you to examine whether you can do it only by yourself. Individuals with Asperger Syndrome are notoriously bad judges about our own capacities, and that is where we often get into the most trouble. If others can do some tasks of your job better than you and if these are not critical skills to learn, let them do it.

Was This a Sound Goal or Was It Something That Just Struck My Fancy at the Time?

The reason why you want to manage your own case should not be just to manipulate your way through a passing fancy. If there is any chance you do that regularly, you have some important personal work to do. You might fool people a few times, people who want to help you, but once you do it more than a few times, the only person you end up kidding is yourself. People who can help, people who really want you to succeed by getting more control over your life, do not like to be played with. Much as bad agencies get a "reputation on the street," self-deluded clients get a reputation as well. Once you gain such a reputation, important decision-makers may not take you seriously, no matter how much you change afterwards.

There is nothing wrong with seeking the help of advocates, mentors and allies to get you where you want to go. One of the most important rules for yourself as you relate to providers in an instrumental way is to ask, "How am I doing?" at each important step along the way. First, ask this of yourself. Then, ask others. The test of being successful is when you become open to honest, nonjudgmental feedback.

How Is My Exit Going to Look?

The way you conclude a case management relationship says a lot about you. The mark of true professional case managers is how they conduct themselves throughout the course of their business dealings. Good case manager know that how successfully a case is completed with one provider augments their reputation "on the street" with other providers. With each successful "close," good case managers builds good reputation and good will capital.

How you finish is every bit as important as how you commence your relationship with providers. In fact, it is more important. Closings, just like openings, leave lasting impressions. Make sure your last impression is a good one.

Roger Meyer *lives in Gresham, Oregon, a Portland suburb. During his 26-year career as a union cabinetmaker, he volunteered evenings and weekends as a young-adult counselor, community organizer, apprentice instructor and community mediator. At the age of 56 he left cabinetmaking to work full time with people.* Author of Asperger Syndrome Employment Workbook, *he is owner of a comprehensive disability case management consulting and advocacy firm "... of a different mind."* Roger facilitates the Portland Asperger Syndrome adult support group and co-facilitates the Portland AS Partners group. He meets monthly with clinicians from multiple disciplines to develop best practices in counseling children, adolescents and adults with AS. Roger is also involved in nondisability community politics. He is a member of the Multnomah County Community Housing and Development Commission and chair of the Rockwood Neighborhood Association.

Recommended Reading

An Aspie's Guide to Understanding Yourself – For Adults
Wendy Lawson has written a do-it-yourself guide to understanding your particular challenges with Asperger Syndrome. Her feedback and self-checking techniques are highly recommended. Over the past 30 years, I have used many of them myself.
  • Lawson, W. (2003). *Build your own life – A self-help guide for individuals with Asperger Syndrome.* London: Jessica Kingsley Publishers.

Modified Cognitive Behavioral Therapy (CBT)
I have been through much bad or ineffectual therapy in my life and still managed to survive somewhat intact. Tony Attwood has written the most comprehensive, single-source description of modified cognitive behavioral therapy known to be effective with AS individuals. Reading this chapter should provide the adult reader with an excellent understanding of CBT. For AS individuals seeking a professional counselor, consider using Dr. Attwood's description of this therapy as a "shopping guide."

- Attwood, T. (2003). Cognitive behavior therapy (CBT). In L. Willey (Ed.), *Asperger Syndrome in adolescence* (pp. 38-68). London: Jessica Kingsley Publishers.

Basic Cognitive Behavioral Therapy Explained, Including Techniques
Aaron Beck is considered the founder of cognitive therapy. Combined with the Attwood chapter above, this book by Beck's daughter and professional colleague is an excellent primer for counselors wishing to be introduced to the nuts and bolts of this counseling approach.
- Beck, J. (1995). *Cognitive therapy – Basics and beyond.* New York: The Guilford Press.

Understanding and Practicing Professional Attitudes
This college text and workbook for young adults in marketing, business management and career exploration classes contains excellent tips and exercises on developing a professional business attitude. I wish I could have gone through some of these exercises years ago.
- Chapman, E., & O'Neil, S. (1999). *Your attitude is showing – A primer of human relations (and self-paced exercise guide)* (9th ed.). Upper Saddle River, NJ: Prentice Hall.

Business Meetings: What to Do When There Are More Than Two of You
While there are more current, comprehensive books on the market, Doyle and Straus' basic book remains among the best books on meetings. When I first started "doing meetings," this book largely replaced *Roberts' Rules of Order* for me. It made more sense than any formal rule book. It has gone through numerous reprintings.
- Doyle, M., & Straus, D. (1993). *How to make meetings work – The new interaction method.* New York: Penguin Putnam Inc.

The Science and Art of Negotiation
This slim volume is the negotiator's Bible. For Aspies, it is a logician's dream come true, backed by nearly three decades of the Harvard Project's sound research. Professional mediators live by its observations. The book is used by many university schools of business and management.
- Fisher, R., Ury, W., & Patton, B. (1991). *Getting to yes – Negotiating agreement without giving in* (2nd ed.). New York: Penguin Books.

Understanding Conflict – A Positive View of Conflict's Role in Power Relationships and Problem-Solving
Conflict and disagreement is inevitable in case management relationships. This college text presents a readable guide to working positively with conflict in work and personal relationships. While it is a bit "college textbookish," it treats conflict with respectful, readable language.

- Wilmot, W., & Hocker, J. (1998). *Interpersonal conflict* (5th ed.). Boston: McGraw Hall.

Advice to Others Interpreting Your Behavior
There is no better guide than this to help professionals "managing" your case to understand the role behavior plays in communicating with AS adults who have expressive language challenges. Herb Lovett was a consumate, humane professional who helped Autism Network International founders get off and running. This book is a "must read" for counselors.

- Lovett, H. (1996). *Learning to listen – Positive approaches and people with difficult behavior.* Baltimore: Paul H. Brookes.

Dual and Multiple Relationships in Professional Settings
This Internet article succinctly describes ethical issues faced by clinical psychologists. Many of the questions and steps in the author's model apply equally well to all client-professional settings where there is a power differential between parties.

- Gottlieb, M. C. *Avoiding exploitive dual relationships: A decision-making model.* Retrieved April 12, 2004, from http://www.kspope.com/dual/gottlieb.php.

CHAPTER 5

Building Alliances: Community Identity and the Role of Allies in Autistic Self-Advocacy

Phil Schwarz

I n this chapter, we will shift gears a bit. Much of this book is concerned with *individual* self-advocacy – in other words, becoming an effective advocate for oneself. But there is also another kind of self-advocacy: *collective* self-advocacy. Collective self-advocacy is about effecting change in how autistic people[1] and autism in general are perceived and responded to by the mainstream society. This chapter explores how we can be effective in collective self-advocacy.

Effecting that kind of change in mainstream society may seem like a daunting challenge, but it is not beyond our reach if we proceed "with a little help from our friends," to paraphrase John Lennon. It is achievable as a gradual, grass-roots change, if we can effectively enlist sup-

---

[1] In this chapter, we will use the term "autism" to refer to the whole autism spectrum, and the term "autistic people" to refer to people anywhere on the autism spectrum. "Person-first" language ("person with autism" rather than "autistic person") may be favored by other disability groups, but it does not make sense with respect to autism. As we will discuss later in this chapter, autism involves central aspects of identity. It is fundamental to who we are, not something we have that somehow can be removed, resulting in a "normal," nonautistic person. It makes no more sense to refer to an autistic person as a "person with autism" than it does to refer to a man as a "person with masculinity." As for the use of the term "autism" to refer to the whole spectrum, we are concerned in this chapter with goals and approaches that benefit all of us collectively, wherever we are on the spectrum.

port and participation from the sympathetic nonautistic family members and friends in our lives acting as allies to us as self-advocates.

Working together, we can win people who have open hearts and minds over to our perspectives a few at a time. Over time, the spread at the grass-roots level of such changes in individual perspective will ultimately change the broader public perception of autism and autistic people, and reframe the issues in terms that are more favorable to us. And even before that process fully works its course, the outcome of individual situations can be improved by the active presence of allies who truly share our perspectives and goals.

In order for any of that to happen, we have to build that network of allies. We have to define what it means to be an ally – to us as autistic individuals, and also to us as self-advocates. We have to identify potential allies among those who live, work, and play with us and care about us. And we have to articulate constructive roles and activities in which those potential allies can engage that will further our goals as self-advocates.

This chapter is intended to be a set of beginnings towards those ends. It is intended to serve as a frame of reference, a source of some comparisons, and a roadmap for the start of an unfolding journey. The chapter is meant to be read both by those of us on the spectrum engaging in self-advocacy and by the sympathetic nonautistic family members and friends who could be effective allies. Please share the information with everyone who cares about you and who might be able to rise to the challenge of seeing things from your perspective and of adopting your goals as a self-advocate as their own.

A Bit of Personal Perspective

My own background and pathway into self-advocacy has given me a dual perspective, that of potential ally as well as that of self-advocate. I am both a parent of an autistic child and an adult on the autism spectrum myself.

In February 1994, my three-year-old son Jeremy was diagnosed with PDD (pervasive developmental disorder). As it happened, the first neurologist who saw Jeremy was British-trained. As seems to be the case among British clinicians, he used the term "Asperger Syndrome" to refer to any high-functioning form of autism. Asperger Syndrome was a new term for my wife and me at the time, so we started reading. As we read about it, we realized that *my* developmental history – that of a smart, weird, socially naive kid with sensory phobias and narrow, intense, encyclopedic interests who developed dysthymia (chronic minor depression) in late adolescence was a "milder" version of what we were reading about Asperger Syndrome.

With the encouragement of the psychologist I had been seeing for dysthymia – the last and longest in a series of therapeutic relationships stretching back 17 years into my college days – I sought a diagnostic consult. And indeed, "mild" AS turned out to be the right description for what I was dealing with. (It could be called "mild," presumably, because I had managed to get through college and several years of employment and the beginnings of a marriage without crashing and burning. But I had begun that 17-year trek through outpatient psychotherapy in college to help me skate around the edges of a nervous breakdown in my junior year. And I had learned over the years to conceal, suppress, and avoid as much as I could of anything for which I might be considered weird or clueless. Not a particularly secure way to live.)

The diagnosis turned out to be a watershed. So many previously seemingly unrelated aspects of my developmental history now fit like puzzle pieces into a coherent frame. I began to forgive myself for the social blunders I had not been able to avoid. But more important, as I met other adults on the spectrum in the course of seeking answers and support, I discovered the degree of intuitive resonance I had with them, not so much in the specific things that interested us or that we enjoyed, but in the *manner* in which that interest or enjoyment played out. I began to learn to cherish and take pride in how my mind worked and in what spoke aesthetically to me and to my fellow travelers, even if unjustly and incorrectly dismissed by the mainstream as meaningless. This began to heal my long-wounded self-esteem better than 17 years of psychotherapy ever could have. I promised myself that I would do whatever I could to spare Jeremy such a long painful trek through self-awareness, as it kicked in for him.

Autism, even high-functioning autism, comes in a bewildering variety of individual experiences. Jeremy's autistic mix is different from mine. Where I was hyperlexic (having taught myself to read at age four), he has significant language-based learning disabilities and delayed development of theory-of-mind reasoning skills. Therefore, self-awareness will probably kick in much later for him and more slowly than it did for me. He will also have intellectual hurdles that I did not have. Nevertheless, self-awareness will come for him, and in the meantime I want to do what I can to change the landscape of mainstream attitudes towards autistic ways of thinking, feeling, sensing, and *being* for the better.

More than self-esteem is at stake here. Because of the prevailing mainstream attitudes towards autism, society spends resources towards the eradication of potential future autistic people that would be better put towards improving the quality of life of autistic people here and now. Prevailing mainstream attitudes stand in the way of recognizing and mitigating the ergonomic, social, and economic obstacles and barriers to long-term employment of people on the spectrum in capacities that best leverage their talents. Prevailing mainstream attitudes dismiss our way of being, our preferences, and our aesthetic sensibilities as meaningless and disordered, and that shortchanges our potential for interacting with the mainstream society and for contributing to it.

A Bit of History

The autism self-advocacy movement is a small voice in the world of autism. Parent and professional groups are larger, better funded, and get most of the media attention. They, not we, tend to shape public perception of autism. That public perception is fraught with misperception. Our message as self-advocates and as those who are living the life gets lost or never heard.

How did this come about? It's a complicated story with many factors. In fact, historically, there are *two* layers of misconceptions about autism for us to overcome, not just one.

Two Layers of Mischaracterization

The parent groups have long been fighting the battle against the first layer, the mischaracterization of autism at the hands of traditional psychoanalytic schools, most notably the charlatanism of Bruno Bettelheim (e.g., Pollak, 1998). That first layer of misconception characterized autism as a psychiatric disorder caused by parents, in particular mothers – and the parent groups and their advocates, with understandable motivation, focused on debunking that misconception. In some countries, such as the United States, that battle is mostly won; in others, such as France, it is still ongoing.

However, that wave of parent-driven energy mobilized against the first layer of misconception sowed the seeds of the second layer. In their zeal to debunk the psychoanalytic-based mischaracterizations of autism by proving the existence of its organic origins, the parent activists of the last four decades have allowed – even leveraged as expedient – a second mischaracterization of autism, a characterization of autism as a disease like any other: a monolithic pathology to be responded to, and battled, and Cured Now[2] and Defeated Now![3] as if it were like any other organic disease – cystic fibrosis, muscular dystrophy, even cancer. Much of the fundraising and media-leveraging apparatus of the big parent-run autism organizations is focused on that mischaracterization, because it produces publicity, funding, heightened priority for medical research and progress towards prevention and cures – results that are appropriate for those other organic diseases. If the formula works for cystic fibrosis or muscular dystrophy, then it should work for autism – or so goes the argument.

But autism is different from those organic diseases, because it is pervasive and involves aspects of us that go way beyond physiology. It involves aspects of us that are fundamental to our identity as human beings: personality, temperament, processing of emotions, sensory preferences, aesthetic sensibilities, and cognitive style. Life-threatening or disabling organic diseases such as macular degeneration, muscular dystrophy, or cancer have profound psychological impact, but they do not pervasively shape identity and individuality in the way that autism does.

Many of the aspects of our identity that are shaped by autism are not intrinsically disordered. They may be atypical. They may require significantly different teaching and child-rearing approaches. They may even put us at an ergonomic, economic, or social disadvantage in conventional society. But they are not all intrinsically defective. Often it is society's intolerance or lack of accommodation, rather than anything intrinsic to the autistic characteristic itself, that renders the characteristic disabling. For instance, what is so intrinsically *wrong* about hand-flapping, about narrow and unusual knowledge interests, about an aesthetic sensibility attuned to repetition or detail rather than holistic gestalt, or objects rather than people? It is society's reaction to these things – society's devaluation of them – that renders them disabling.

---

[2] Cure Autism Now (http://www.canfoundation.org) is one of the major parent-run autism organizations. For an autistic person's perspective on the approach Cure Autism Now and similar organizations take towards autism that is shared by most self-advocates, see
http://www.autistics.org/ library/love.html
[3] Defeat Autism Now! (http://www.defeatautismnow.com) is the current project of Bernard Rimland, a leading figure in the wave of parent activism beginning in the 1960s that, much to his and their credit, overthrew the psychoanalytic misconception of autism as a psychiatric condition caused by bad parenting. However, as explained in the course of this chapter, the characterization of autism as a monolithic organic disease to be responded to like any other organic disease is also a misconception, with its own adverse consequences.

Of course, autism is not about just these aspects of identity and atypical individuality. Many autistic people experience characteristics of autism that *are* intrinsically disabling, sometimes profoundly so. For example, they may lack means of oral or written communication. They may lack basic personal hygiene skills. They may lack the ability to make effective judgments on safety issues. They may lack control over impulse-driven behavior. They may suffer intractable sensory distress.

It is difficult for parents and family of autistic individuals who are profoundly disabled in such critical respects to see autism as anything *but* those critical disabilities. This is particularly true of parents of children who appear to be developing normally up to a certain age and then begin to lose skills. It sure sounds and feels and is *lived* like something that is 100% bad and, therefore, worthwhile attempting to eradicate 100%.

However, as even autistic individuals who are profoundly disabled eventually gain the ability to communicate effectively, and to learn, and to reason about their behavior and about effective ways to exercise control over their environment, the unique individual aspects of autism that go beyond the physiology of autism and the source of the profound intrinsic disabilities will come to light. These aspects of autism involve how they think, how they feel, how they express their sensory preferences and aesthetic sensibilities, and how they experience the world around them. Those aspects of individuality must be accorded the same degree of respect and the same validity of meaning as they would be in a nonautistic individual rather than be written off, as they all too often are, as the meaningless products of a monolithically bad affliction.

The truth for all of us, at all points on the autism spectrum, lies between the extremes: There are both intrinsically disabling factors in autism, and aspects of atypical individuality that are disabling primarily because the society devalues them or fails to accommodate them.

Why the Second Mischaracterization Is Problematic

If autism is characterized as a monolithic pathology, then to "cure" an individual of autism – to eradicate all autistic features in an individual – would involve not just mitigating the truly intrinsically disabling aspects of autism, but also erasing and overwriting the aspects of the individual's identity that are affected by autism. The end result would no longer be the same person. This is why Temple Grandin said (as quoted by Oliver Sacks, 1995): "If I could snap my fingers and be nonautistic, I would not – because then I wouldn't be me. Autism is part of who I am" (p. 291).

Jim Sinclair, in his landmark essay *Don't Mourn For Us* (1993), states this in starker terms:

> *Autism is a way of being. It is not possible to separate the person from the autism. Therefore, when parents say, "I wish my child did not have autism," what they're really saying is, "I wish the autistic child I have did not exist, and I had a different (non-autistic) child instead."*

> *Read that again. This is what we hear when you mourn over our existence. This is what we hear when you pray for a cure. This is what we know, when you tell us of your fondest hopes and dreams for us: that your greatest wish is that one day we will cease to be, and strangers you can love will move in behind our faces. (http://www.ani.ac/dont_mourn.html)*

Most parents balk at that last image. Most parents would say that they have no such intention, that they love their child and would never even think of giving him or her up for a different child. But if they do not grasp that autism entails so much more of an individual's very essence than neurophysiology or handicap or learning disability, they will not understand that a true "cure," a complete eradication of autistic features, would in fact leave them with a different child – not just metaphorically different in terms of abilities, but literally different in identity and personality.

Eventually, it does become clear to many parents whose children are making progress in overcoming the intrinsically disabling factors they face that autism is more than just those intrinsically disabling factors. It becomes clear to them that autism involves both intrinsically disabling factors and atypicalities closely bound up with individual identity that are not in and of themselves disabling, but only become so because of how society devalues them or fails to accommodate them. Most of those parents will start to rethink their notions about what it means to seek blanket prevention and cure of autism. They learn to focus instead on what it takes to mitigate specific disabling factors and remove specific barriers – whether that involves changes to the individual or to the individual's surroundings, and by extension, society. They start to see the notions of cure and prevention differently – more like we do.

On a larger scale, they begin to see that the species is enriched by the variety that autistic atypicalities represent when the profoundly disabling factors are mitigated or accommodated. They begin to see that prevention and cure – eradication of autistic features and their sources in the gene pool – would eliminate not just the profoundly disabling factors, but that very variety in the species, leaving it unquestionably poorer.

The Challenge We Face

The question before us, then, as activists in the autism world – whether as parents, professionals, or self-advocates – should not be how to *eradicate* these atypicalities, but how best to *enable* individuals with these atypicalities: what mix of change *in the society*, as well as change in the individual, should we strive for?

This question requires a significant rethinking of the goals and fundraising activities of much of the establishment of major autism organizations, at least as expressed and implemented at present. An organizational apparatus geared around an exclusively pathological model of autism as a defect in the individual, for which the appropriate response is solely to fix the individual, through intervention, prevention and cure, fails to consider – or even ask – this important question.

The very vocabulary, verbal and emotional, of the intervention- prevention-and-cure approach demeans and undermines us as self-advocates. Pity, helplessness, and tragedy juxtaposed against intervention, prevention, and cure as the antidotes to them are the elements of this second mischaracterization of autism that is the stated mission of many of the biggest, best organized, and best funded autism organizations and foundations. There is no room in that approach for self-advocacy. Instead, the implicit message to us as self-advocates is, in effect, "sit down and be quiet – don't get in the way of the marketing model."

So how can we proceed and get our message heard as self-advocates in such a climate and landscape? With a little help from our friends – from a population of potential allies far larger than us in numbers.

The question is, "How do we identify and mobilize that population of potential allies?" The answer may come from the experience of other groups that similarly have had to overcome massive public misperception – in particular, groups that have an identity/membership pattern similar to ours, a pattern I call "unconventional diaspora."

A Bit of Demographics

Conventional diaspora or minority groups – ethnic, religious, racial diasporas and minority groups – have a family-based identity/membership pattern. Whole families belong to the group, or not. Whether or not an individual ultimately chooses to identify with the group or dissociate from it, that individual generally was born into a family belonging to that group. For example, one is born Jewish or Irish or African-American, for the most part, into a family that is Jewish or Irish or African-American.

In contrast, unconventional diasporas have an individual-based identity/membership pattern. That is, most members of such groups belong to families in which most of the other family members are not part of the group. Disability and gender orientation tend to work that way: The gay community and the Deaf community, for example, consist mostly of members who come from predominantly heterosexual or hearing families, respectively. The autistic population is also such an unconventional diaspora. That is, most autistic people come from mostly neurotypical families.

This sets up a dynamic regarding advocacy and activism that is significantly different from that which exists for conventional diasporas and minority groups. There is an important extra party in the equation: family members who are not themselves members of the unconventional-diaspora group. What should be their role? What can be their role? If the members of the unconventional-diaspora group do not articulate an agenda for them, others may do so to the detriment of the group. In our case, the prevention-cure agenda and the second layer of public misperception about autism have been the results.

Some unconventional-diaspora self-advocacy communities have identified, and defined, and are working to support, a constructive role for family members. This role has great potential to turn the tide of public perception and align family agendas with those of the unconventional-diaspora group members themselves. It is the role of ally.

The Role of Ally

Simply put, an ally is someone who is not a member of the unconventional-diaspora group himself or herself, but has the motivation to learn and understand the group's issues and perspectives and to work to further the group's agenda.

Family members, who are often powerfully motivated by love for their family member who is a member of an unconventional-diaspora group, can make good allies. The love they feel for their family member may be powerful enough for them, with the right encouragement, to reject adverse public perceptions and "conventional wisdom" about the unconventional-diaspora group. It may be powerful enough for them to listen instead to what the group members are saying themselves, and to act upon that deeper, truer knowledge.

For example, some family members of gay people often rethink life-long beliefs about homosexuality, sometimes courageously bucking pressure to the contrary from family, community, and tradition, to arrive at a place of acceptance of their gay family member (see, for example, http://www.familyacceptance.com, the Family Acceptance web site). Some family members of Deaf people undertake to learn American Sign Language to be able to fully communicate with their Deaf family member and his or her friends in the Deaf community on their own terms – and to appreciate and take part in the rich culture of the Deaf community.

These family members, these potential allies, have to be reached not only with the group's perspectives, message, and agenda, but often before that with a preliminary message. That preliminary message is the notion that there could even *be* a set of perspectives and an agenda, of, by, and for the group itself, that is at variance with the broader public perception and conventional wisdom.

The Deaf community has struggled long and hard to establish this notion as it pertains to deafness and Deaf people in the mind of the general public. That struggle has met with some degree of success, particularly after the watershed student protests in March 1988 that led to the appointment of the first Deaf president of Gallaudet University ("Deaf President Now – 15th Anniversary," http://pr.gallaudet.edu/dpn.). The tide for the gay community's perspectives began to turn with similar historic watershed events such as the Stonewall rebellion ("The History of the Stonewall Rebellion," http://eserver.org/gender/stonewall-history.txt) and the removal of homosexuality as a category of psychiatric illness from the *Diagnostic and Statistical Manual of the American Psychiatric Association*.[4]

The notion that we as autistic people have a set of perspectives and an agenda that is at variance with the broader public perception and conventional wisdom is something of which families of autistic people are often completely unaware. This is not so out of malice, but simply because our voice as self-advocates is so small amid the cacophony of voices, perspectives, and theories that exists about autism, generated almost entirely by people who are not themselves autistic. When they *do* encounter our perspectives and agenda, and their points of variance

---

[4]For an eloquent perspective on how homosexuality was removed from the DSM as a psychiatric disorder, listen to the installment of the Public Radio International documentary *This American Life* titled "81 Words" (http://www.thislife.org/pages/descriptions/02/204.html).

with the broader public perception and conventional wisdom, it is sometimes somewhat of a shock.

Family members also have to be reached with the notion that they, as nonmembers of the group, could possibly have – *should* have – a constructive role to play in the group's self-advocacy efforts, adopting and promoting the group's agenda – as *allies*. This latter notion is critical.

So finding and developing allies among family members can involve a good bit of work, and a good bit of change and growth, for all involved.

How the Role of Ally Spreads and Exponentiates

Once a few such allies are identified and developed, they can help exponentially in identifying and developing further allies. Very often ally-to-other-potential-ally outreach can accomplish more in less time than group-member-to-potential-ally outreach because the shared experience between the parties is closer.

In the community of families with autistic children, parent-to-parent sharing of experience and bonding is a powerful mechanism. It is vitally important for parents who *do* understand the aims and goals and validity of autism self-advocacy to reach out to other open-minded parents. Some of that is happening with word-of-mouth interest spreading among parents who have read Valerie Paradiz's wonderful book, *Elijah's Cup* (2002). A landmark in autism literature, it is perhaps the first parent's narrative to take seriously not only the perspectives of individual autistic adults, but the very existence and validity of autistic community and culture, and the critical role the latter can and should play in the development of healthy self-esteem in autistic kids.

Over time, a quiet, steady increase mounts in the portion of the total population who is willing to challenge the established public perception and conventional wisdom, and, ultimately, the established public perception and conventional wisdom are toppled. This transformation of public perceptions has happened regarding issues pertaining to so many populations within our diverse society, ranging from religious, cultural, and racial differences to gender issues to disability issues. It is just as sound a model for the transformation of public perceptions of autism.

The principal components in this game plan for quiet revolution are twofold. The first component is initial outreach and education by self-advocates to a core set of allies. The second component is subsequent ally-to-potential-ally outreach and education alongside continuing group-member-to-ally communication.

Other Groups' Histories and Models to Follow

We can learn a great deal from the inroads other unconventional-diaspora groups have made before us in two key areas. First, inroads they have made into articulating an agenda that challenges the mainstream conventional wisdom. Second, inroads they have made into defining the role of ally and building alliances and networks of allies. The Deaf community, in particular, has pioneered notions of positive group identity and cohesion, and group culture. These notions are relevant models for the *messages* we want to empower allies to help us bring to the mainstream society's perception of people on the autism spectrum and their needs and place in society. The gay community, in turn, has pioneered effective models for *defining* what it means to be an ally, and for *identifying and empowering allies*.

Activism in the Deaf Community

The history of activism in the Deaf community is worthwhile for us to examine for several reasons. The Deaf community is one of the best organized and cohesive disability populations. Like the autistic population, the Deaf population is an unconventional diaspora. That is, Deaf individuals typically belong to hearing families, just as individuals on the autism spectrum typically belong to families that are by and large nonautistic.

The Deaf community has long had a vision and agenda for optimal outcomes for Deaf people that are at variance with the conventional wisdom about disability. The model for which the Deaf community has sought to win acceptance is commonly referred to as the social or cultural model. It focuses on accommodations the larger society should make to enable Deaf people to function as full members of society *as Deaf people*. These accommodations include captioning of video programming, sign language interpretation of speech and song at public events and increased sign language fluency in the general public, better visual signage in public places and buildings, and visual augmentation of auditory signals such as bells and alarms.

In contrast, the conventional wisdom about Deafness on the part of the hearing general public is that it is a disability, a deficiency, something that must be corrected or repaired in the *individual* in order for that individual to take part in the larger society. Thus, according to the conventional wisdom, the onus is upon the individual to change, not society. This is commonly referred to as a pathological or medical model of disability.

Much of our own agenda as autistic self-advocates centers around a similar distinction between the pathological model of disability and the social model of disability. It emphasizes the need to shift public attention and conventional wisdom, resources, and funding from goals that are motivated by an exclusively pathological-model view of autism, to goals that are motivated by a view that takes the social model of disability into account as it applies to autism. In other words, a shift from goals of cure and prevention to goals of greater accommodation of the sensory and social needs of autistic people, and greater acceptance of autistic sensory and social preferences, aesthetic sensibilities, and cognitive styles as fully valid and meaningful strands in the fabric of a diverse society.

Alexander Graham Bell, familiar to most people as the inventor of the telephone, was also active in efforts to develop approaches to educating Deaf and hard-of-hearing children and integrating them into the larger society. In his day and age, there really was no alternative to the pathological model. His approach focused on teaching Deaf people to lip-read and vocalize, and to fit in to the extent they could as handicapped members of a hearing society. Approaches that diverged from the goal of fitting into a hearing society without demanding any accommodations from it were discouraged. Not only was the notion of attempting to get the larger society to accommodate Deaf people by provision of signed interpretation and other visual devices that the general public would not need considered preposterous, the very teaching and use of sign language among students in Deaf schools was prohibited.

This approach flourished in Bell's lifetime, and for decades beyond. Even today, the Alexander Graham Bell Association for the Deaf and Hard of Hearing remains a major player in the Deaf and hard-of-hearing establishment. It continues to promote the use of spoken language by Deaf and hard-of-hearing people, although not to the exclusion of the teaching and use of sign language, as in decades past.

The social-model approach actually has roots that go back as far as Bell's approach. The National Association of the Deaf and countless local organizations of Deaf people have as long a history as the Bell Association. Theirs is a contrasting history, however, one of activism with the goals of promoting sign language as a legitimate means of communication among and with Deaf people; promoting video captioning, teletype phone service, visual augmentation of auditory alarms and signals, and other assistive technologies; promoting Deaf community cohesion and culture; and promoting parity and equity within the larger society for Deaf people as Deaf people.

Through the 1980s and 1990s, the Deaf community made good progress with the social-model approach despite the continued entrenchment of the Bell approach. High points in that progress included the aftermath of the national publicity around the successful Deaf President Now protests at Gallaudet University,[5] and the passage of the Americans with Disabilities Act. Assistive technology and wider acceptance, support, and fluency in American Sign Language proved able to provide better outcomes for Deaf people than auditory- and speech-based strategies aimed at fitting into the hearing world without accommodations. Much of this progress came about through joint activism on the part of Deaf people and of allies to the Deaf community in academia, government, disability law, and the wider disability community. In fact, the Deaf President Now protests themselves succeeded because of the support of allies that the students had among the faculty, alumni, and the community outside the university.

Recent advances in the technology of cochlear implants, a surgical technique that combines electrodes surgically implanted in the inner ear that stimulate the auditory nerve with outboard microphone pickup and sophisticated speech-processing electronics, have changed the landscape somewhat. Cochlear implant technology does not provide full-range hearing (and it does not help people with loss or profound damage to the auditory nerve itself), but with the latest refinements in the technology, it apparently produces signals varied enough to permit discrimination of most speech sounds in some Deaf people.

Initially, there was great controversy and resistance on the part of Deaf community activists to cochlear implant technology. Deaf community activists expressed particular resentment over the medical proponents of cochlear implant technology recommending that hearing parents have their Deaf children implanted at ages early enough to predate the typical childhood development of speech acquisition, and then have them educated in an exclusively mainstream, auditory, speech-based environment. Such ages are much earlier than children could give any legitimate sort of informed consent themselves. Moreover, children placed into exclusively mainstream educational environments would grow up totally disconnected from the Deaf community. Deaf activists felt that this practice could lead to the eventual disappearance of Deaf language – sign language – and Deaf culture.

---

[5] These were protests initiated by students, and then joined by faculty and alumni, at Gallaudet University, perhaps the premier university for Deaf and hard-of-hearing people in the United States and the world. The protests were over the university board's decision to choose a hearing candidate for the university presidency, passing over qualified Deaf candidates. See "Deaf President Now – 15th Anniversary." http://pr.gallaudet.edu/dpn

More recently, some degree of rapprochement seems to have taken place between the Deaf-culture and Bell camps, with a mutual consensus that Deaf children and adults should be given every opportunity to live and socialize in both worlds – the Deaf community and the mainstream society.

However, the challenge remains for Deaf activists and their allies to prevent new forms of pathology-model "conventional wisdom" from taking root in the larger society. Among these is the mistaken notion that cochlear implants can now "fix" deafness and that, therefore, the extensive inroads the Deaf community has made towards establishing assistive technologies and accommodations on the part of the larger society are no longer necessary. Another such mistaken notion is the idea that because cochlear implants can give some Deaf people the means to navigate hearing and speech-based mainstream society, Deaf community and culture themselves, as distinct entities separate from mainstream culture, are no longer necessary, legitimate, or desirable.

The response of the Deaf community and Deaf activists to this new challenge will be relevant and instructive for us, as autistic self-advocates, to watch unfold. Although the history of autism interventions is littered with short-lived fads and overhyped or oversold approaches and products, the current pace of research may lead to developments that impact our agenda as self-advocates as profoundly as cochlear implant technology has impacted the Deaf community and its agenda.

The Role of Allies in the Gay Community

The gay community is the group that has best developed the role of ally and models for action on the part of allies, in ways that can benefit us as autism self-advocates. Regardless of one's feelings towards the gay-rights movement, it is instructive to examine the issues that the gay community identified as needing action, and how it leveraged the role of ally and developed networks of allies to address those issues.

A Google search on phrases such as "what it means to be an ally" or "how to become an ally" yields numerous hits on web sites of gay university student organizations. These sites feature well-thought-out definitions of the role of ally, checklists and examples of how allies should (and should not) behave, issues on which allies can make a direct impact, and announcements of seminars and workshops for training prospective allies.

Once again: as you read through this section, try to set aside your opinions regarding homosexuality itself – whether positive or negative. Instead, try to see how many parallels you can find between issues that these organizations have identified as needing action, and issues confronting autistic people. Try to see how much of the definition of ally, and how many of the roles for allies these organizations have identified, readily apply to potential allies of autism self-advocacy and autistic people.

Some of the definitions of the role of ally that these organizations have adopted include:

- An ally is "a person who is a member of the dominant or majority group who works to end oppression in his or her personal and professional life through support of, and as an advocate for, the oppressed population" (Washington and Evans, "Becoming an Ally," referenced in "What Is an Ally?," Eastern Michigan University LGBT Resource Center, http://www.emich.edu/lgbtrc/resources/ally.html).

- An ally is someone who is not gay, lesbian, bisexual or transgender (GLBT) but personally advocates for GLBT equal rights and fair treatment ("Coming Out as a Straight Ally," Human Rights Campaign Foundation, http://www.hrc.org/ncop/straightallies/index.asp).

- Allies are individuals who are willing to provide a safe haven, a listening ear, and support for lesbian, gay, bisexual, and transgendered people or anyone dealing with sexual orientation issues. ("Aggie Allies," Texas A&M University, http://allies.tamu.edu/ default.htm).

Some sites and sources further expand the definitions of the role.

Who are allies? **Allies are people who:**

- Voluntarily designate themselves as a "safe person" who will maintain confidentiality and offer support to the GLBT community.

- Believe that it is in her/his life-interest to be an ally.

- Acknowledge and articulate how patterns of fear have operated in her/his life.

- Recognize and appreciate the struggle that is a part of establishing a positive lesbian/gay/bisexual identity.

- Attempt to contest and overcome subtle and pervasive oppression and insensitivity (Eastern Michigan University LGBT Resource Center).

What does it mean to be an ally?

- An ally validates and supports people who are different from themselves.

- An ally realizes and questions personal privilege and uses it to benefit people who are oppressed.

- An ally examines their own prejudices and is not afraid to look at themselves.

- An ally supports the oppressed group's voice and sense of autonomy.

- An ally works with the oppressed group, offering support by being accountable to, but not being responsible for, the oppressed group.

- An ally emphasizes action.

- An ally is an advocate when the oppressed group is absent by challenging (mis)conceptions.

- Being an ally means: sharing the power, taking a risk, taking responsibility, opening yourself up to the unknown, realizing that you are part of the solution, leveling the playing field, accepting differences, making allowances, and leading by action (Western Washington University, Prevention and Wellness Services, "What Is an Ally?" http://www.wwu.edu/chw/preventionand wellness/allypages/whatisally.html).

Some sites and sources further clarify the role by identifying behavior that is not part of, or consistent with, the role of ally:

An ally is NOT:

- someone with ready-made answers

- necessarily a counselor, nor is he/she necessarily trained to deal with crisis situations

- expected to proceed with an interaction if levels of comfort or personal safety have been violated ("What Is An Ally?," Eastern Michigan University LGBT Resource Center, http://www.emich. edu/lgbtrc/resources/ally.html).

How GLBT allies do NOT act:

- They don't assume heterosexuality

- They don't hold stereotypical beliefs about GLBT people or about the concept of "family"; they don't think their own view of reality is the only view of reality

- They don't make jokes or slurs about GLBT people

- They don't omit GLBT people from art, TV, books

- They don't assume that they are more competent than GLBT people

- They don't take responsibility, think, or speak for GLBT people

- They don't assume that one GLBT person represents the whole group

- They don't trivialize the concerns and issues of GLBT people; they don't ignore GLBT issues

- They don't expect GLBT people to educate them about culture

- They don't *expect* to be trusted by GLBT people

- They don't regard GLBT culture as underdeveloped or disadvantaged

- They don't turn to GLBT culture to enrich humanity while simultaneously invalidating it by calling it exotic

- They don't ignore the effects of homophobia and heterosexism

- They don't get offended when they are assumed to be GLBT (Eastern Michigan University LGBT Resource Center).

A number of sites and sources describe seminars and "advances" for prospective allies to educate them about being allies and about the issues on which they can help as allies. The term "advances" was chosen in contrast to "retreats" to imply forward rather than backward motion (Allies Advance FAQs, Texas A&M University http://allies.tamu.edu/ advances.htm; Allies Program, U. of Central Florida, http://www.counseling.sdes.ucf.edu/AlliesInfo.html; Establishing an Allies Program, Human Rights Campaign Foundation, http://www.hrc.org/ncop/ allies/print.asp).

The issues that GLBT students and student organizations face, and around which they have sought to enlist and empower allies, include:

- Ignorance or misinformation among the mainstream population about the origins of homosexuality and the behavior and views of homosexuals

- Historically and culturally rooted prejudice against GLBT people

- Intolerance of homosexual behavior, in particular of social and romantic behavior by homosexuals that would be considered matter-of-fact and natural between heterosexuals

- Overt acts of homophobic hostility, harassment, and violence

- Inequity in legal, economic and health benefits

- Discrimination in housing, employment, and membership or participation in public organizations and activities

Allies can help in the struggle with these issues in a number of ways:

- By working to develop an understanding of homosexuality and of how these issues impact GLBT people, they can work at a grass-roots level, person-to-person, to dispel the misinformation and historically/culturally based prejudice.

- They can intervene in situations where homophobic labels, remarks, or jokes are made to counteract the tacit approval and reinforcement such behavior tends to get from the passivity of most bystanders.

- They can intervene in, or report, overtly hostile, harassing, or violent behavior against GLBT people.

- They can demonstrate, petition, and provide testimony in efforts to get laws and public policies changed.

- They can provide solidarity in numbers: There are far more non-GLBT people in mainstream society than there are GLBT people. There is strength in numbers, and in endorsement of the GLBT community's positions by significant numbers of outsiders.

- They can enlist and empower even more allies within the mainstream population – sometimes more effectively than GLBT people themselves.

- And finally, they can be "safe people," way-stations in the incremental and sometimes scary or risky process of GLBT individuals coming out:

    The process of coming out is one of enlarging a series of concentric circles of those who know. Initially the process should be in control of the individual until (and if) they consider it public knowledge (Eastern Michigan University LGBT Resource Center).

What We Can Learn from These Models as Autistic Self-Advocates

The Deaf community's history of organization and cohesion as a community can serve as a model for us, as a community of people on the autism spectrum and as self-advocates. The Deaf community's articulation and advocacy for a social-model approach to Deafness can likewise serve as a model for us, as we articulate the changes we seek in mainstream attitudes towards autism and mainstream accommodation and acceptance of our sensory, aesthetic, and social needs.

Identifying as a community, and identifying and articulating a common agenda that counterbalances the exclusively medical/pathological model of autism that holds sway in the conventional wisdom of the mainstream population, are necessary preliminary steps to building a network of allies. We have to be able to articulate the vision for which we are seeking our allies' help in bringing to acceptance, and ultimately to prevalence, in the mainstream population.

The gay community's experience also serves as a model for us in the steps that follow – the actual identification and empowerment of allies. There is a significant degree of parallelism between gay experience and issues and our own as people on the autism spectrum. Gay groups have done extensive work developing the role of ally to gay people, and in developing an agenda for allies to gay people that furthers gay self-advocacy goals. Their work can be directly applied to developing a role of ally to people on the autism spectrum, and an agenda for allies to people on the autism spectrum that furthers our goals as autism self-advocates.

From the Deaf Community: Identity as a Community and Social-Model Agenda

In order to effectively self-advocate, one needs to develop a healthy self-esteem. This is as true on the group or community level as it is on the individual level. We must be able to see ourselves as a coherent group with a common set of interests and shared experience.

In Chapter 1, Ruth Elaine Hane describes the experience of being on the "outside looking in." But we have our own cultural context, our own "inside." Those of us who meet other autistic people in person or over the Internet discover that common ground.

The Deaf community's history can point the way. The Deaf community became a coherent community through a shared language, through shared educational experience, and through shared community experience continuing into adulthood. Sign language is the shared language. Education in schools for the Deaf is the shared educational experience. Signed and captioned arts performances, social functions, and community events, along with participation in local Deaf community organizations, comprise the shared community experience continuing into adulthood.

This shared experience as a community enhances the sense of the group as a healthy, vibrant community with a legitimate *culture*. It also enhances the self-esteem of individuals as fully capable human beings, when allowed to function in environments that support their natural means of communication and patterns of socialization.

What parallels can we apply to the autistic population? While there is not a direct parallel to the single strong, unifying cohesive force that sign language plays in the Deaf community, there is a significant body of experience that we as folks on the autism spectrum share. For example, we tend to develop deep, encyclopedic interests in specific subjects or topics. While we may not develop those interests in the same subjects or topics, we have in common the *process* and *patterns* by which we do so. While we may not have in common the specific details of the sensory diets we seek and the sensory stressors we avoid, we have in common the process and patterns by which we do so. While we may not have in common the specifics of our individual flavors of autistic aesthetic sensibilities and cognitive patterns, we have in common the process and patterns by which they have come about and developed. While we may not have in common the specifics of how we navigate our own corner of the overwhelmingly nonautistic social world around us, we have in common the process and patterns by which we learn to do so, and by which we attempt to deal with the hurdles we face in that regard. Finally, while we may not find the same specific jokes funny, we share *patterns* of humor based around wordplay and unexpected juxtaposition of structure.[6] These shared patterns and shared experiences comprise a *culture*, every bit as much so as Deaf culture and gay culture.

There is much to talk about with one another regarding how we make our respective way in the world, and gathering together as a community is the way to do so. And gathered together, there is strength in numbers: more stories, more patterns corroborated and harder for the

---

[6] When my autistic son Jeremy was four years old, after the eleventh-third replay of his favorite Raffi video, with the song "I love to ate, ate, ate, ay-pples and ba-nay-nays," Jeremy slyly looked at me and began to sing: "I love to seven, seven, seven ..."

mainstream society to continue to ignore. As a recognized group, it becomes easier for our testimony about the *meaningfulness* of our aesthetic sensibilities, our cognitive styles, our emotional language, and our socialization patterns – our *culture* – to be taken seriously by the mainstream.

Deaf history goes back decades before the advent of instantaneous written telecommunication via the Internet. It involves the establishment of local Deaf clubs and social organizations, and the struggle to get teletype-based assistive technology applied to the telephone network. Nowadays, e-mail, instant messaging, and other forms of instantaneous written communication abound, and they are transforming the social patterns in the Deaf community.

As autistic self-advocates, we came into the picture as a community at the dawn of the era of the commercially available Internet. Many of us use the Internet to find and correspond with fellow travelers and to become part of a far-flung community. The Internet is a great boon to those of us who find it easier to communicate in editable, near-real-time writing than in real-time speech. It is a vital alternative for those of us who find the sensory environment of face-to-face social venues stressful and inhibitory. Our community is still so small and far-flung that contact through the Internet augments and sustains the face-to-face gatherings that we do have, and assists us in producing traditional written material such as articles and books.

One commonality we have with the Deaf community lies in the notion that we do have shared experience, shared culture, that is different from that of the majority. Writing and speaking about that shared experience helps establish its – and *our* – legitimacy in the eyes of the majority.

Another commonality we have with the Deaf community is the value of articulating a social-model approach to our existence, to counterbalance the medical/pathological-model approaches created about us (but almost entirely *not by* us). That social-model approach should identify concrete sensory and social accommodations that the mainstream society should be obliged to make for folks on the spectrum. It should advocate acceptance of our aesthetic sensibilities, cognitive patterns, emotional responses, and socialization preferences as diversity issues – establishing neurological diversity as a legitimate dimension of diversity alongside religious, ethnic, racial, gender, and physical-ability diversity in the mainstream society. Such a social-model approach can be particularly important in gaining and maintaining access for us in higher education, employment, housing, and a host of other areas that directly affect our quality of life.

That social-model approach should start with the basic notion that people on the autism spectrum are not merely "broken" neurotypical people who need to be "fixed." As in the story of the *Ugly Duckling*, we are in some respects swans rather than broken ducks,[7] with our own strengths and abilities that require accommodation and acceptance of diversity on the part of the mainstream society in order to blossom to full value. A cornerstone of our agenda as communal self-advocates should be the message that it is not just the individual who needs to change, but society as well.

From the Gay Community: The Role of Allies

Just as the Deaf community can provide us with relevant models for community cohesion and a collective agenda, the gay community can provide us with relevant models for developing a network of allies.

We can begin by drawing the parallels that exist between some of the issues the gay community faces and some of the issues our community faces, and by examining the gay community's development of the role of ally.

As autistic self-advocates, we face some issues that parallel some of the issues facing gay people, around which GLBT organizations have sought to enlist and empower allies:

- Misconceptions about the nature of autism (as a disease one has, and not in any way as an integral part of the identity and personality that one is)

- Misconceptions about the mental capabilities, powers of observation, and feelings of people on the autism spectrum

- Misunderstanding and intolerance of autistic behavior, in particular odd but harmless sensory behavior, and behavior that does not follow mainstream social expectations

- Denial of the legitimacy of (and meaning innate in) autistic cognitive styles, emotional responses, aesthetic sensibilities, and sensory and social preferences

---

[7]A metaphor articulated beautifully with respect to us folks on the spectrum by Bob Morris, of the Greater Georgia Chapter of the Autism Society of America, and by Lisa Cohen, of the Asperger's Association of New England, in their writings and spoken presentations.

- Overt acts of harassment and violence, including bullying and taking advantage of naiveté

- Inequity in legal, economic, and health benefits – as disabled people in general, and as people with an "invisible" disability that does not involve tangible accommodations such as wheelchairs or Braille signage

- Discrimination and exclusion from employment opportunities and advancement

Allies to autistic self-advocacy can help in the struggle with these issues in a number of ways that closely parallel the ways in which GLBT organizations have enlisted the help of allies to GLBT people. For example, allies to autistic self-advocacy can:

- Work to develop an understanding of autism spectrum conditions on a social-model basis as something we are rather than something we have (which, once somehow removed, would render us "normal" neurotypical people).

- Learn how the issues above impact us, then work at a grassroots level, person-to-person, to dispel the misconceptions and to challenge the exclusive dominance of the medical/pathological model of autism.

- Intervene in situations where hostility, harassment, unfair advantage taking, and even violence are perpetrated against people on the spectrum, and counteract the tacit approval and reinforcement such behavior tends to get from the passivity of most bystanders.

- Demonstrate, petition, lobby, and provide testimony in efforts to get corporate and public policies changed.

- Provide solidarity in numbers. There are far more nonautistic family members and friends than there are autistic self-advocates. Their numbers add to our strength, and their endorsement of autistic self-advocacy positions and perspectives amplifies the weight and clout of those positions and perspectives in the mainstream society.

- Enlist and empower even more allies within the mainstream population, sometimes more effectively than autistic self-advocates can do so themselves. For example, parents can sometimes share perspectives with other parents in ways in which autistic self-advocates who are not parents cannot.

- Function as "safe people" in the process of disclosure. For those of us on the autism spectrum who manage (or struggle) to "pass" in employment or other public social situations, disclosure is often as complicated and risky as coming out is for GLBT people. Allies who can fully grasp the complexity and nuances in the process of disclosure can serve as "safe people" for those of us on the spectrum in the same way that allies to GLBT people serve as "safe people" in the process of coming out.

Where Do We Go from Here? Some Practical Thoughts and Points

How do we begin the process of identifying and empowering allies in our own life circumstances and communities? Here are some suggestions.

- First things first: Get clear on the agenda, so that you can articulate it and educate potential allies about it. The Resources section at the end of the chapter lists some sources on social-model approaches and advocacy of a sensible *mix* of mitigating disability in the individual and removing barriers in the society.

- To identify potential allies, consider the same set of concentric circles of people to whom you might disclose your status as a person on the spectrum. People closest to you – people to whom you can safely and comfortably disclose the most about yourself – are probably the best to start with as potential allies. They will form your core set of *personal* allies.

- Review the disclosure and information-sharing activities that Liane Willey describes in the next chapter. Consider how many of them could be accomplished with the assistance or participation of one or more trusted people – friends, family, whomever. Those folks are all potential personal allies! Get them exposed to the alternatives to the medical/pathological model of autism and to the idea that society as well as the individual has to change in order to maximize our outcomes.

- Remember that good allies can *themselves* help identify and empower additional allies, once they are "on message." Once you have a few personal allies, people you can safely and comfortably disclose to and work with, ask them to get involved in mainstream autism organizations – local organizations, or even regional or national organizations, if they're able to – and spread our messages and recruit more allies. In their chapters of this book, Kassiane Sibley (pp. 57-61) and Liane Willey (pp. 187-188) offer several suggestions for how to increase public awareness of *our* perspective on autism and on the needs of autistic people that both self-advocates and allies can implement.

- Begin to consider specific areas in which allies can intervene more effectively than we can as self-advocates. Here are some examples (which have strong parallels in gay-community ally programs):

    - Have allies learn how to effectively intervene in bullying and harassment situations in school or recreational settings – how to combat the passivity of bystanders that empowers the perpetrators.

      Allies can be very effective in helping to break cycles of bullying, harassment, and discriminatory behavior. Ruth Elaine Hane uses the notion of front- and back-stage behaviors (pp. 21-22) as a model for what goes on in bullying, and for that matter in "adult" equivalents of bullying – acts of harassment and discriminatory behavior.

      Most nonautistic children develop a good intuitive sense of when their behavior is being witnessed (front stage), and by whom, and when it is not (back stage). Bullies rely on the absence of witnesses with the authority to stop or punish their behavior, and on the silence of those who do witness their behavior. Allies can break the cycle by being there to witness and to speak up. Often just the mere knowledge that someone who will speak up is watching is enough to deter bullying and its "adult" analogues.

–   Have allies in the workplace get involved in planning and
    training around sensitivity to diversity and accommodation
    of diversity in the workforce.

    Most mid- to large-size employers have programs in place
    addressing other kinds of diversity – racial, religious, ethnic,
    gender, perhaps even gender orientation (gay/straight). Work
    with potential workplace allies to open those programs to con-
    sidering neurological diversity and the needs of employees on
    the spectrum. Issues to consider include sensory needs, educa-
    tion of nonautistic coworkers about autistic social preferences,
    and identification and development of alternative means of
    team-building and other group-socialization activities that
    respect the needs and preferences of employees on the spec-
    trum and do not disenfranchise them.

–   Have allies get involved as "safe people" in the disclosure
    process.

    Starting on page 22, Ruth Elaine Hane builds an effective
    model for making personal-disclosure decisions. On page 24,
    she identifies the role that a "helpful person" can play in dis-
    closure situations. This is exactly what we mean by "personal
    ally," and facilitating successful disclosure is one of the funda-
    mental roles that allies can take on. Nonautistic allies can help
    autistic people working through disclosure situations both by
    helping them understand the perspectives and likely reactions
    of the nonautistic people being disclosed to, and by "paving
    the way" – by working with the people being disclosed to, to
    identify and change adverse preconceptions they may have
    about autism and autistic people.

    Allies can do this important work as individuals, but also
    (and sometimes more effectively) as a team. Often, allies
    working together as a team can be more effective in "paving
    the way" for safe and successful disclosure.

–   Parents who become allies can be effective in an absolutely
    critical role – teaching self-advocacy skills to their autistic
    children.

Kassiane Sibley's chapter is a must-read for parents and others who want to act as allies in that role. Kassi teaches us something very important: that self-advocacy can occur in one form or another at all stages of life and at all levels of development. It is far from being an activity that only those of us with speech and a full set of independent living skills can engage in. As parent or caregiver allies, there is a crucial role to play in enabling and facilitating self-advocacy, at whatever level and scope the autistic individuals in your life are capable of – or become capable of – progressing over time

As Stephen Shore discusses in his chapter of this book, teaching children how to effectively contribute to developing their IEP is an important goal and a concrete example of the ally's role in teaching self-advocacy skills. It will help build a foundation for self-advocacy in postsecondary education and/or employment.

– Roger Meyer alludes to yet another constructive role for allies in Chapter 4. That role is to help identify and interpret the rules of organizations, social systems, and social environments in which autistic people have to function, and with which we have to interact.

Ultimately, the ideal is for each of us to become our own case manager, to the greatest extent possible, and hence to internalize that process of observation and interpretation. However, that end-goal of internalization involves a learning process, and allies can play an important constructive role in enabling that learning process. This is true both for allies acting in a professional capacity as counselors, and for allies acting in a "lay" capacity.

On page 137, Roger mentions pilot projects. Yet another area in which allies can help, particularly as their number, interconnectedness, and clout increase, is in identifying, publicizing, and directing business to pilot projects whose goals are in harmony with our interests as self-advocates. This kind of activity is also helpful in bringing market forces to bear upon uncooperative agencies and providers when more cooperative alternatives to them exist.

One final, extremely important point:

- There is one thing that is really important about being an effective ally that is often lost on nonautistic family members who are active in mainstream autism organizations, or in providing or advocating for education or employment of kids (or adults) on the spectrum. That is the essential and critical quality of a true ally that an ally does *not* serve as an effective ally by implementing his or her own agenda or ideas about what people on the spectrum need. Rather, a true ally implements *the agenda of the people to whom they are an ally.*

  Sometimes parents, educators, professionals, advocates, or clinicians, with the best of intentions, think of themselves as "allies" to people on the spectrum because of all the work they have done in the field that surely must be beneficial. In most cases, they *have* done a great deal of significant work that has benefited people on the autism spectrum. However, being an ally in the sense we have been talking about in this chapter is different: It is about listening to the agenda and perspectives of people on the spectrum *themselves*, and acting to implement *their* agenda and bring the mainstream around to *their* perspectives. That may require setting aside quite a bit of one's own agenda, perspective, and maybe even ego. This can be difficult to do, but very worthwhile and rewarding because by doing so, one is truly empowering the people to whom one professes to be an ally.

Conclusion and a Call to Action

The trails that have been blazed for us to some extent by the Deaf and gay communities represent new territory for both self-advocates and allies. The sky is the limit, and the opportunity to effect a subtle, gentle, beneficial revolution in the way mainstream society treats people on the autism spectrum is beckoning, waiting for us to embark on the journey together and to get started working together as self-advocates and allies.

More power to us all in that endeavor. Send me postcards from the journey as you proceed. My e-mail address is in the resources section that follows.

Phil Schwarz *is vice president of the Asperger's Association of New England (AANE), and has been a member of Autism Network International (ANI) since 1994. His chapter in this book is the outgrowth of workshops he has led on the role of allies in autism self-advocacy at Autreat 2003 (the annual conference/retreat of ANI), at the 2003 national conference of the Autism Society of America (ASA), and at a joint conference of the Maine chapters of AANE and*

ASA in March 2004. He is doubly involved in the autism community as an adult with a mild variant of AS and the father of a high-functioning autistic son. Professionally, Phil is a software architect and developer.

Resources

Readings on Autism as Fundamental to Identity
- Baggs, A. (1999). *Two Book Reviews.*
  http://www.autistics.org/library/reviews.html
- Meyerding, J. (1996 to date). *Snippets.*
  http://staff.washington.edu/mjane/snippets.html
- Meyerding, J. (1998, rev. 2002). *On Finding Myself Differently Brained.* http://staff.uwashington.edu/mjane/diff.html
- Meyerding, J. (2002). *The S Word (and Why I Hate It).*
  http://staff.washington.edu/mjane/shy.html
- Meyerding, J. (2003). *The Autistic Way of Being in the World.*
  http://staff.uwashington.edu/mjane/way.html
- Meyerding, J. (2003). *The Great "Why Label?" Debate.*
  http://staff.uwashington.edu/mjane/label.html
- Sinclair, J. (1993). *Don't Mourn for Us.*
  (http://www.ani.ac/dont_mourn.html)
- Sinclair, J. (1999). *Why I Dislike "Person-First" Language.*
  http://www.jimsinclair.org/person_first.htm

Readings on the History of Public Responses to Autism and Social-Model Alternatives to the Medical/Pathological Model of Autism
Author's note: some of the readings in this section and the next convey (with justification) a good deal of anger at the current state of near-

invisibility of *autistic* voices, perspectives, and priorities in the political landscape of autism, and at the powers maintaining (or attempting to maintain) that state of affairs. If you are a nonautistic but sympathetic parent, family member, friend, or provider, please don't reflexively assume that *you* are being attacked, as you read. You have the very real opportunity to become part of the solution, part of the way forward from this current state of affairs.

- Baggs, A. (2000). *Love, Devotion, Hope, Prevention, and Cure.* http://www.autistics.org/library/love.html
- Baggs, A. (2003). *Rewriting History for Their Own Ends: Cure Autism Now and The Mind Tree.* http://www.autistics.org/library/tito-can.html
- Baggs, A. (2004). *Then and Now.* http://www.autistics.org/library/thenandnow.html
- Dawson, M. (2003). *Bettelheim's Worst Crime: Autism and the Epidemic of Irresponsibility.* http://www.sentex.net/~nexus23/md_01.html
- Klein, F. (2002). *Build the Autistic, Don't Tear Him Down: A Clarification of My Opinions Regarding Teaching Autistics How to Live.* http://home.att.net/~ascaris1/build.html
- Paradiz, V. (2002). *Elijah's Cup: A Family's Journey into the Community and Culture of High-Functioning Autism and Asperger's Syndrome.*
- Schwarz, P. (1995). *Cure, Recovery, Prevention of Autism?* http://www.autistics.org/library/pschwarz.html
- Schwarz, P. (2002). *Book Review:* Elijah's Cup *by Valerie Paradiz.* http://www.autistics.org/library/elijahscup.html
  Included in this list primarily for its summary of four fundamental principles embodied in Paradiz's narrative in *Elijah's Cup* (and based on a social-model approach to autism) for raising autistic children so as to develop strong self-esteem as *autistic people*, and so as to develop into effective self-advocates
- Sinclair, J. (1992). *What Does Being Different Mean?* http://www.jimsinclair.org/different.htm
- Sinclair, J. (1995). *Medical Research Funding?* http://www.jimsinclair.org/research.html
- Sinclair, J. (1998). *Is "Cure" a Goal?* http://www.jimsinclair.org/cure.htm
- *Stop Pity Website.* http://www.stoppity.org. A perspective from neuromuscularly-disabled self-advocates on what is problematic

about the mass fundraising approach of the Muscular Dystrophy Association and its Jerry Lewis Telethon, a general model that is considered a "gold standard" by most mainstream autism organizations.

Readings on the Validity of Autistic Opinions, Perspectives, and Agendas
- autistics.org (2004). *In Support of Michelle Dawson and Her Work.* http://www.autistics.org/library/dawson.html
- Baggs, A. (2000, rev. 2003). *The Validity of Autistic Opinions.* http://www.autistics.org/library/autopin.html

Readings on Combating Bullying and Harassment
- Dixon, M. (1999 to date). *Raven Days Website.* http://www.ravendays.org
- Heinrichs, R. (2003). *Perfect Targets – Asperger Syndrome and Bullying; Practical Solutions for Surviving the Social World.* Shawnee Mission, KS: Autism Asperger Publishing Co.

Readings on Accommodations in the Workplace
- Walker, T. (2003). *Square Pegs: Autism in the Workplace.* http://home.earthlink.net/~mellowtigger/conf/ SquarePegs 20031002.html and http://home.earthlink.net/ ~mellowtigger/conf/SquarePegs-20031002.ppt

General Sources on Autistic Self-Advocacy and Autistic Self-Advocacy Agendas
- Autism Network International (1997, rev. 2002). *Introducing ANI: Philosophy and Goals.* http://www.ani.ac/intro.html
- Baggs, A. (1999). *The World I Want to Live in.* http://www.autistics.org/library/want.html
- Klein, F. (1997 to date). *Autistic Advocacy Website.* http://home.att.net/~ascaris1

Readings on the History and Principles of Deaf Community and Culture
- Gallaudet University Office of Public Relations. (2003). *Deaf President Now – Fifteenth Anniversary.* http://pr.gallaudet.edu/dpn
- Schein, J. (1989). *At Home Among Strangers.* Washington, DC: Gallaudet University Press.

Sources on Ally Programs
- Eastern Michigan University LGBT Resource Center. (2004). *What Is an Ally?* http://www.emich.edu/lgbtrc/resources/ally.html
- Human Rights Campaign. (2004). *Coming Out as a Straight Ally.* http://www.hrc.org/Content/NavigationMenu/Coming_Out/ Get_Informed4/Straight_Allies/Coming_Out_as_a_Straight_All y2.htm
- Texas A&M University Department of Student Life. (2004). *Aggie Ally.* http://allies.tamu.edu/default.htm
- University of Central Florida Counseling Center. (2004). *The Allies Program at the University of Central Florida: Official Mission and Vision Statement.* http://www.counseling.sdes.ucf.edu/ AlliesInfo.html
- Western Washington University Division of Student Affairs and Academic Support Services. (2004). *Ally Building Network.* http://www.wwu.edu/chw/preventionandwellness/ allypages/allybuilding.html

- My e-mail address: pschwarz@ix.netcom.com

References

Paradiz, V. (2002). *Elijah's cup: A family's journey into the community and culture of high-functioning autism and Asperger's Syndrome.* New York: Simon & Schuster Free Press.

Pollak, R. (1998). *The creation of Dr. B.* New York: Touchstone Books.

Sacks, O. (1995). *An anthropologist on mars.* New York: Alfred A. Knopf.

Sinclair, J. (1993). *Don't mourn for us.* www.ani.ac/dont_mourn.html Also in Autism Network International newsletter, *Our Voice,* Volume 1, Number 3, 1993, and in 1993 International Conference Proceedings, "Autism: A World of Options," Toronto: July 14-17, 1993, Autism Society of Canada and Autism Society of America, 155-158.

CHAPTER 6

Disclosure and Self-Advocacy: An Open Door Policy

Liane Holliday Willey

I am a too-much-information (or TMI) kind of Aspie. This sort of tell-all personality comes very naturally to me. From the moment I could string three words together, my father has said when asked about my character, "Tell Liane; tell the world." I readily admit he had cause for making such a statement. I vividly recall more than one moment of tell-all that must have left my parents' cheeks as red as a bullfighter's cape. For example, my mother loves to tease me about the time I let her guests know that the cake they were enjoying had been dropped on the floor just minutes before they arrived for dinner. Even though she had told me not to tell anyone she was going to be serving a dirty cake, I could not help but tell! It did not bother me the cake was dirty, it was just too much to keep the information a secret.

I often wonder what it would be like to be a more still sort, the kind of person who walks in mystery and keeps quiet better than an icebox keeps cold. My friend and a contributor to this book, Ruth Elaine Hane, is quiet. The first time I met her, I was awestruck by her grace and control. She moves like a smooth cat, and her voice is as soft as a purr. In many ways my personality is the direct opposite of hers. Her chapter in this book examines the toughest inner struggles that come when we on the spectrum try to express who we are and what we need. I urge the more quiet of you to look longer at her chapter than at mine, as you determine what kinds of disclosure issues you have to contemplate. If you are a more active and loud Aspie, one who is at the point in life where you feel it is time to have more fun than furrows, my chapter is for you.

Like most louder-type Aspies, I find that my interests are exactly what I need to talk about, and I have loads of stories to tell, lots of eccentricities to express and plenty of laughs to share. Whenever I am among a group of people, I head toward the nearest corner to recite my favorite monologues. I remember a Super Bowl party one year when I was fixed in my favorite corner of a favored friend's home. I was surrounded by my two best caregivers at the time – Margo and my husband, Tom. With them literally and figuratively on my side, I started my monologue. Within minutes, everyone listening to me was laughing. I was telling a story that involved me, a new car, an abandoned dog I was trying to rescue, a locked garage, a locksmith, and rows of scratches on the new car.

Suffice it to say, it was a good story that almost told itself. To me it was exactly the kind of story that bears repeating, even though I am made to look like a total fool. Indeed, I was the fool in the center of the tale, so why not admit it, especially if being a fool can be so funny! It is that kind of storytelling that leads most people who know me to say that I can be as silly as a stand-up comedian. I like that comparison, and I know that if I ever thought about censoring myself, I would have no show to put on, and that thought is intolerable to me. I love being on stage, making people laugh and think and cry. In fact, there is nothing I love doing more.

In thinking about this, it dawns on me that there may be a real Aspie reason why I like being able to influence how a person feels. If I can make someone laugh, for example, chances are good that he or she is feeling happy. If I can make a person cry, on the other hand, it is likely that I have provided feelings. Voila! No more trying to figure out how somebody's feeling!

Is it egomaniacal for me to want to monologue? Is it rude for me to only want to talk about things that interest me – things I can readily understand and relate to? I do not think so. I think it is simply an organic response to my need to control my environment and, therefore, interact with it appropriately. If left on its own, the world gets too jumpy and chaotic. I cannot handle that kind of environment. I need predictability and "certainess," or as my husband says, I need to have things carved out in stone.

I used to deny that fact was my reality, but once I started openly disclosing my AS, I found it immensely easy to assert my needs by saying things like, "I hate to sound like a control freak, but my AS works a lot better for me if I can have some say in what the day will be like. So, do you mind if I help make the plans or if I reserve the right to reject what you want to do?" Friends who know me do not even have to hear this plea. They immediately ask me if my needs are being met. Folks I have just met who remain interested in being my friend after hearing such a statement quickly express their understanding and acceptance. Others I meet look startled and wander off and out of my life. That makes me extremely uncomfortable. It seems I will never get used to the feeling that I am unwanted, or worse, misunderstood.

I would much rather be a communications dictator than a passive listener. It suits the Aspie in me just fine. Consequently, it should come as no surprise that I am a walking, talking, breathing billboard for Asperger Syndrome awareness. There is no one and no place I find off limits when it comes to my own personal disclosure, especially when that disclosure whirls around something as important as Asperger Syndrome. I have told everyone – from complete strangers in the middle of a grocery store aisle, to old high school friends at our twentieth reunion – about my AS.

If you were to ask my children how appropriate my disclosures are, they would tell you, "not at all." But if you ask me, I would say that they are extremely important. Case in point: Would it have been better for the young woman pushing her cart by me in the grocery store to believe she and her young children were in the company of a kook escaped from Kookland when they came upon me in the middle of the canned fruits and vegetables aisle happily singing made-up songs about the friendship between green beans and corn, or was it more appropriate for me to explain to her, as I did,

"Oh my! I must seem pretty strange to you right now. Goodness. I'm not really. It's just that I have a unique personality that stems from something called Asperger Syndrome, and part of my Asperger Syndrome gets kind of goofy in loud public places, so to calm myself down I try to have fun and close myself off from things around me. Hence, the singing. When I am singing and concentrating on making

*rhymes and rhythms about whatever I am looking at, say green beans
and corn, I can forget the chaos in the grocery store. And I imagine
that until the world sets out to calm down the chaos it creates, I'll be
singing to cans and just about anything else I see when I am out and
about in the world."*

OK, so my kids might be right. Perhaps I did not need to tell the
woman a thing about my singing. Certainly, I did not owe her an expla-
nation. But I think my actions were well worth the effort. In my mind, I
did the right thing because in so doing I can be sure that at least the
woman came away from the ordeal (a) realizing I was not a harmful kook
and (b) having acquired a bit of awareness about Asperger Syndrome.

Now, this does not in any way imply that I think everyone should be
as open about their AS as I am. We owe it to yourselves to be as loud or
as quiet as we want to be regarding every aspect of who we are, especially if part of who we are is something as difficult to understand as AS.

The ideas I present in this chapter are not well suited for all Aspies;
however, I think there is something for everyone. Do not hesitate to
make modifications or additions. Play with the ideas and make them
work for you.

There are two parts to my AS awareness plan. The first is disclosure
for its own sake; the second is self-advocacy. While one can happen
without the other, I find the two join to form an incredibly strong bond
from which many positive things can build. Think back to my experience with the young woman at the grocery store. Perhaps my explana-
tion of why I was singing to canned goods helped her think about how
annoying loud and chaotic environments can be. Taken a step further,
perhaps her realization would lead her to express to the grocery store
manager how nice it would be to have soft white noise in the background to mask the sounds of clanging cans and bottles, crying babies
and whinny pushcart wheels. At the very least, perhaps my telling the
young woman who I was (the disclosure) coupled with the telling of
what I needed (the self-advocacy) helped her consider that sometimes
there is a rhyme and a reason behind what appears to be odd behavior.
In short, maybe my disclosing and then advocating for a change helped
someone accept people with differences.

Disclosure

I chose long ago to have fun with my Aspieness, especially when it comes to my disclosures. I spent too many years hyperventilating and wiping away tears. Far too many. It is much better for my peace of mind, not to mention my health, to remain as upbeat and lighthearted as I can when I talk about AS. If I do not, I am liable to sink into a hole of self-doubt, and worse, self-pity. I have come close to that hole many times, and it is not a pretty place.

I remember one occasion when I found myself asking a distant relative why he was always so mean to me. He told me he never meant to be mean to me, and that I was taking him too seriously and not realizing he was just kidding with me. Ah, so that was the problem. I did not realize when he was kidding with me – I am an Aspie and that is extra hard for me. "Oh! So you were kidding all those times you told me I was just a 'little bit' too tiny to worry about. Those were kidding words! To think I spent all that time bellied up to the dinner table just so I would be big enough to worry about." Sure, I could have stayed angry, but what good would that have done? It was much healthier to laugh and move on. But it was most healthy for me to share my AS with this relative. Only after he learned about my AS, I figured, would he be able to understand how vulnerable I am to mixed messages.

Telling my relative about AS was relatively easy (no pun intended!). Telling others can be a lot more complicated. In an attempt to keep disclosure as simple as possible, I came up with the following disclosure strategies.

Host a Coming-Out Party

- Include your favorite and your least favorite snacks, labeling each as either an acceptable or an offensive food, so that guests can get an idea of how finely tuned your gustatory senses are likely to be. I like very crunchy foods layered with all sorts of spices, so I would naturally have those in big bowls to illustrate their importance in my diet. I hate soggy foods like custard and hummus, so those foods would sit in tiny bowls to symbolize their lack of importance.

- Provide an Aspie-friendly party atmosphere by drawing attention to the things that make you particularly comfortable and calm. For me, that would mean I would place loads of soft blankets and pillows on my furniture and in corners of the room; I would put extra rugs on the floor to keep extraneous noise down; I would have soft instrumental music playing; and I would light dozens of no-scent candles to create a soft atmosphere without nasty smells. Also, there would be politely worded little signs posted about the house suggesting everyone use library voices, respecting personal space and not smoking.

- Give Aspie-approved stim toys to guests for party favors. Smooth rocks, kaleidoscopes, stretchy rubber toys, and yo-yos would be in bags I would provide. If you do a web search for "sensory toys," plenty of addresses will pop up, making it easy to find such goodies.

- Plan ahead and write away for copies of AS newsletters and support group information fliers that you can put on tables and in the bathroom. Set out books, videos, and ASA audiotapes. Supplement the information with your own fliers or brochures that include your favorite web sites, research sites, support centers, and any personal Aspie information you would like to share.

- Make your own Aspie version of the classic *Twenty Questions* game. Rather than classifying your idea as either an animal, vegetable, mineral or other, suggest the following: sensory integration, cognitive processing, social skills, emotional concerns, and language issues.

Just the Facts, Ma'am

Fans of the 1950s detective show *Dragnet* will recognize the Aspie-like response of Sergeant Joe Friday whenever he encountered someone trying to present too much information. Take Friday's advice, and let the facts of AS be the core of your AS disclosure. Much like you might discuss the differences between contact lenses and glasses, or the merits of good ethics over cheating, you can simply put forth the differences between neurotypical and AS. Just be sure to include somewhere in the discussion the point that you are Aspie!

Send the News

Kassiane Sibley shares my notion that successful disclosure and advocacy can also be accomplished through various forms of writing. It is often less daunting to explain complex issues in writing than in spoken dialogue. Today's printing software programs and the mass marketing of scrapbooking supplies make it easier than ever to create home-made cards, announcements, fliers, brochures, and even books. If it is too much of a struggle or an inconvenience to explain your AS verbally, put your creative talents to use and design self-published material you can send to the people you think should understand your AS. Depending on the mood you are most comfortable with, make your publication anything from informal and light via a flier, to something more formal and elegant via a card, to a newsy bunch of facts and information via a newsletter. Whichever medium you choose, consider including an invitation to discuss AS in more detail through e-mail or traditional U.S. mail letters. For even more ideas on using letters and newsletters to disclose AS information, see Kassiane's chapter, particularly pages 48-54.

Find an Agent

Phil Schwarz talks about how important it is for the autistic community to have strong allies in mainstream society. I share Phil's belief that it is imperative to have strong and long-lasting allies, or agents, as I call them, to help us in our quest to make Asperger Syndrome and autism better understood. In fact, I am inclined to think that one of the most nonthreatening ways to disclose your AS is to find a trusted friend to serve as your ambassador or agent. Arm the person of your choice with more than enough AS information that he or she can subsequently share with people you have identified as those who need to know. Provide your "agent" with a list of things he or she should feel free to discuss on your behalf.

In my case, my agent tells our mutual friends that it is difficult for me to socialize too much, hard for me to read their friendship cues, and that it is not typical for me to invite others to my home. This serves the dual purpose of preventing me from having to constantly explain myself and letting others know I am not nearly as odd or unrefined as they might think. The agent idea also serves to help me build a few close relationships between the person who speaks on my behalf and myself. That is the best benefit of all!

I remember the first time I realized that benefit. About five years ago, I overheard (my excellent hearing is another trait I attribute to my AS) a group of women expressing to one another their inability to understand how our mutual friend, Margo, could be such a good friend of mine. I told Margo what the women had said, and she immediately expressed both her anger at the women and her concern for my hurt feelings. From that moment on, she had very little to do with that group of women, and even more to do with me. And whenever we came upon the women in the small town we all shared, Margo would make it very clear that I was her closest and most fun friend.

But she went further than that. She also set about telling others about AS and the effect it had on my sensory system and my language. When Margo, one of the most respected individuals in our tiny community, started disclosing my AS and advocating for my needs, people listened and learned. Some even grew to like me despite their earlier inclinations to disregard me, but none ever developed a bond with me like Margo did.

Self-Advocacy

Disclosure to those who matter the most makes life a much better place to visit, but if you want to really live a full life, you have to work hard to make others accept and understand your AS. As my father so often reminds me, you have to be your own press agent. In short, you have to be a self-advocate. Roger Meyer does a great job of breaking down the rudimentary elements involved in acting as your own best case manager in his chapter. I urge you to study his advice and then combine it with my advice below. In that way, you will be certain to have a very complete understanding of adult Aspie self-advocacy.

To begin your advocacy work, do as much as you can to really understand who you are, because before you can do a complete job of explaining who you are and what you need, you must be certain you have those answers yourself. It is not enough for you to know when you were born, where you live, and what your favorite subject matter is. You have to spend some time educating yourself, and then lots of time educating others about AS. Once those roots have taken hold, you can go on to nurture your individual self-advocacy garden.

Understanding yourself in a nonjudgmental way is discussed in further detail when Stephen Shore writes about "Being with Myself" as part of the *Three Worlds of Being* in Chapter 3, and also in Ruth Elaine's chapter.

Self-Analysis

- Gather up and analyze who you are as reported in your diaries and journals. In my old journals, I spent pages explaining how difficult it was to understand my female peers' interest in make-up, appropriate dress, and political correctness. I used up plenty of ink writing down my impatience with my girlfriends' reluctance to say what they really thought, especially when it came to boys in our school. "Why," I once wrote, "doesn't Suzy tell Dave how angry she is with him for not returning her call? She's told me enough times, but isn't he the one who really needs to know?" Clearly, the boy-girl communications dance was lost on me. While most kids knew how to shape their language to fit each unique situation, I used mine to assert my demands. While most kids knew language had the power to make or break a relationship, I thought it was merely a skill that separated us from other mammals.

- Review home movies and pictures and try to interpret how you tend to act around others, what kinds of behaviors you demonstrate, and how others seem to relate to you. I know for a fact that I reacted poorly to events out of the ordinary because I have the pictures to prove it. Virtually every picture taken of me at a special event shows my face yellow from a stomach ache and terrible anxiety. I did not pretend to have a hard time at parties and big events merely to get attention, as some who know nothing of AS might suggest. I experienced a total physical letdown whenever I was in the midst of too much of anything.

- Read as many of your school, medical, and psychological records as you can. See if you can find information that might be useful. For example, your physician might have indicated that you suffer from irritable bowel syndrome when you are overly anxious, and your school records might include a report from a teacher who expressed concern for your happiness on the playground. Reports such as those bring an objective look at your struggles, while underscoring the fact that you are not a wrongdoer looking for trouble, but an innocent bystander in need of a few safeguards.

- Ask friends, family members, and coworkers to give you their impressions of your personality. Reassure them that you want to hear their honest assessment of both your strengths and your weaknesses.

When your self-analysis research is complete, compare and contrast what you discover and look for themes that might express your personality in general, as also discussed in the "Being with Myself" part of the *Three Worlds of Being* in Stephen's chapter. For example, when I researched and then analyzed this kind of information for myself, I quickly saw that others see me as humorous, logical, and intelligent, but also as strong-willed, obsessive, rigid, eccentric, overly analytical, and unorganized.

Determining how others make us feel can be difficult for us Aspies because it requires interpretation of another's subtle verbal and nonverbal cues. More about the me-you relationship can be found when Stephen talks about "Being with Others" and the *Three Worlds of Being* as related to disclosure. My diaries and journals remind me that while I agree with those who see me as funny, unorganized, logical, and rigid, I would not see myself as obsessive, overly analytical, strong-willed, or eccentric. For example, I did not describe my daily 10-mile bike rides as obsessive. Instead, I wrote that my quest for a ride of precisely 10 miles each day was a sign of dedication and drive. I bragged in my journals about my ability to see all sides of a problem just like a lawyer would. I never told myself I was being too analytical. And strong-willed? No way! I often wrote about how I worked harder on a project than most everyone else did and, further, that my ideas about a project were usually better than my peers' because of that hard work. Did I think I was too eccentric? Not at all! I thought my decision to wear turbans and bedtime slippers to school was proof that I was a unique individual worthy of the thespian club I belonged to.

I am convinced that my personality, which is so carefully shaped by AS, appears different only because I stand in direct contrast to the masses who are not as committed as I am to a tenacious understanding and interest in things unique and curious. In other words, I see what some consider flaws in my character as good things worthy of praise. It is all a matter of perspective. And if I want others to see me as I see myself, it is incumbent on me to do my best to arrest any notion that my tenacious manners are signs that I am obsessive, that my desire to deeply analyze is unnatural, or that my unique interests are a sign that I am odd. I have to advocate for who I am by explaining and showing to others that I am a caring individual who has much good to share, despite the fact I wring my hands, speak bluntly, cringe in crowds, cover my ears in loud areas, jump when I am touched from behind … the list goes on. But the fact remains: *People with AS are as real and important as every other human being on earth.*

Educating Others

People can only come to understand the true self of others, if they understand the myriad things that make them tick. It helps when we know someone's general cultural background, a thing or two about their personal belief system, something about their education, and the kinds of things they like to do and think about. AS is part of my cultural background and, therefore, a piece of the puzzle others need when they try to put together who I am.

My favorite Aspie metaphor has me thinking of myself as a giant monster cookie. This kind of cookie has all sorts of goodies in it. I see the organic me as the cookie dough and AS as the chocolate chips, raisins, and oatmeal flakes. And I am, just like the cookie, all the better for having the extra goodies mixed in. When I am done educating others about the good things that come with AS, especially when I have taught them to see us from positive perspectives, I believe others will agree that a giant monster cookie is a nice treat to have around.

I choose to educate others about AS in a rather informal and non personal fashion. My methods illustrated below are steeped in my tendency to tell all, but yours do not have to be. Feel free to borrow, bend, and modify my ideas so that they become yours, for only then will they work … for you.

When it comes to educating others, Kassiane and I share some of the same general ideas. For example, I:

- Send books, journals, and newsletters on AS to the people I am most interested in sharing with.

- Draft letters explaining AS in general to local and national political leaders.

- Communicate with business representatives who offer diversity training to their employees.

- Present AS information to schools and local special education groups.

- Occasionally write articles for the media.

- Invite my family and friends to AS meetings and conferences.

- Take part in autism awareness activities.

The Process of Self-Advocating

Even after people realize I am an Aspie, and even after they have come to understand what Aspie means, they may not have a sense of how integral my AS is to my very being. I think this is because AS is mainly an invisible difference. What we need, and how we get to where we are going, can be hidden beneath a completely normal-looking facade. For example, whereas it would be obvious to sense what a woman might need were she to try out for a position on a sports team made up of males, it would be very difficult for the average person to sense what an Aspie might need in any given everyday situation. Most people would never realize, for example, how difficult it is for Aspies to understand innuendo or sarcasm. Nor would they be likely to quickly fathom how easy it is for Aspies to get totally lost in social mixes that are built on body language and less-than-obvious social rituals.

But who could blame them for their lack of knowledge? Neuro-typicals see the world through their own eyes, just like we Aspies see the world through our own eyes. That is the nature of humans – to relate to life through individual experiences. But whereas we Aspies have loads of places and people to refer to in order to understand neu-rotypical behavior, neurotypicals do not have nearly as many autobi-ographies, movies, novels, textbooks, or even acquaintances, from which they can learn about Aspieland. It is our job, at least it is left to us, to tell – or show – them our needs.

- Decide what you need, who can help you meet each specific need, and how you will explain those needs. I know, for exam-ple, that I need to protect my auditory system from loud noises, so I wear bright orange earplugs most of the time. When I catch someone looking at them, or if someone is brave enough to ask me about them, I simply take them out of my ear to let the per-son see that my bright squishy clay-like earplugs are easy ways to keep noises out. It turns out that most people are more intrigued by the look of the earplugs than the fact I hate noise. And that helps me avoid any embarrassing feelings.

- Decide what has to happen in order for your needs to be met. Be prepared to share your plan with those who can make it happen. I am always careful to ask for plenty of details before I go anywhere new. If I hear a detail that I know will make me nervous, I find a way to keep from coming face-to-face with it. For instance, during the planning of a vacation once, I heard we would be staying in a cabin by a lake where people often went fishing. I was quick to explain to the person making our plans that I did not want to be near a fish smell and that I would appreciate a cabin as far from fish stench as possible. My wish was granted, and I was able to avoid wearing a gas mask the whole trip!

- Make an appointment to meet with the people who need to hear, and then help you, achieve your needs. Do not be late for your appointment, and if you should have to cancel it, call to do so as early as possible. After all, if you are asking for special help, the least you can do is be courteous and timely.

- Practice what you will say. Ask a trusted friend to listen to you and role-play with you what might happen at the meeting. I used to practice what I wanted to say in front of a mirror and using a tape recorder. I would watch my facial expressions and practice making appropriate eye gestures and smiles. Then I would play the tape recording for my dad and ask him to make any suggestions as to how I could improve my thought process or my speech. Together, we would make sure I put my best self forward.

- Dress appropriately for the appointment. This helps to illustrate the fact that your meeting is important. Do not do what I used to do, which was to wear baggy blue jeans and sweat shirts. Instead, look to a clothes catalog to find an outfit you can copy. That way, you will know you are dressed nicely.

- During your appointment, be certain to stay focused and to the point. Do not use your meeting as an opportunity to unload all your frustrations or worries. Use the meeting to express why you have the needs you do and why having your needs met will make a given situation more productive. State your plan calmly and politely. Try to control your impulse to speak impromptu, a behavior I wish I had mastered long before the day I stuck my finger in my mouth and groaned, "Eww, gross," as I came back to a job offer a personnel consultant was trying to get me to me consider.

- Listen respectfully when the person or people at the meeting give their responses. If you feel you do not fully understand something, ask for clarification.

- When the meeting is over, go over what you heard and what you learned. Discuss how you all agreed your plan will be implemented. Compel yourself to express any reservations you may have about your ability to accomplish your side of the plan. I remember accepting a plan that involved me working on a paper with a group of other students. What a disaster! I ended up writing the entire paper and alienating other students at the same time. I should have expressed my dismay over the plan in the beginning. It would have been far better for me to admit my inability to work well with others on anything that involved writing than to even try to participate in the assignment.

- A few days after the meeting, find a way to express your thanks. Depending on the nature of the relationship, you might send a thank-you note, take the person out to lunch, share a hug, or bring the person a bunch of flowers. I routinely write a short e-mail, and I have always been thanked for doing so.

- If it is too difficult for you to express your needs in person, write a letter instead. Be sure to keep the letter to the point, so that your message does not get lost in too much language or too many random ideas. Most etiquette guides suggest that you keep your letter to under the equivalent of one full 8x10" page. That is good advice.

- Share with a friend how the meeting went and what you think it will accomplish. This might reduce your anxiety, and it will give your friend a chance to help make certain you did not mis-interpret something that was said or offered to you.

I feel a sense of pride when I share my AS with others, and I enjoy the feeling of accomplishment when I educate the public about AS. In fact, if I thought my attention-shy family would let me, I would be even more open with my AS news. I would wear "Ask me about AS" buttons and hand out bumper stickers and business cards with my personal web page (http://www.aspie.com) on them. I would introduce myself to people by stating my name and then adding that I had Asperger Syndrome. I might even dress up my dogs with Aspie Pride banners and then walk them in our town's parades.

It is up to you to decide how to disclose and how to self-advocate. My only unwavering advice is that you keep your discussions as positive and optimistic as possible. Take pride in who you are and in what you can do. Then, take heart, for more often than not, the pay-off is brilliant.

Liane Holliday Willey is a Doctor of Education, an internationally respected speaker and writer on Asperger Syndrome, and a researcher who specializes in psycholinguistics and learning-style differences. She has worked as an elementary education teacher, a waitress, a retail salesclerk and a university professor. Following years of improper diagnoses, she was properly diagnosed with residual Asperger Syndrome in 1999. She is the author of Pretending to Be Normal: Living with Asperger's Syndrome *and* Asperger Syndrome in the Family: Redefining Normal *as well as the editor of* Asperger Syndrome in the Adolescent Years: Living with the Ups, the Downs and Things in Between. *She has also contributed to several books on Asperger Syndrome. When Liane is not presenting information on Asperger Syndrome, she is likely to be found at her children's functions, working on her first novel, or consulting with businesses that are interested in building more effective communication paradigms.*

INDEX

D

E

F

G

H

I